HOW TO MOTIVATE
TODAY'S WORKERS

Bernard L. Rosenbaum, Ed.D.

HOW TO MOTIVATE TODAY'S WORKERS

Motivational Models for Managers and Supervisors

McGraw-Hill Book Company
New York St. Louis San Francisco Auckland
Bogotá Hamburg Johannesburg London Madrid
Mexico Montreal New Delhi Panama Paris
São Paulo Singapore Sydney Tokyo Toronto

Library of Congress Cataloging in Publication Data

Rosenbaum, Bernard L
  How to motivate today's workers.

  Bibliography: p.
  Includes index.
  1. Employee motivation. 2. Employee motivation
—Problems, exercises, etc. 3. Psychology, Industrial.
I. Title.
HF5549.5.M63R67   658.3'14   80-27201

ISBN 0-07-053711-9

  3 4 5 6 7 8 9 0   BPBP   8 9 8 7 6 5 4 3 2

The editors for this book were William R. Newton and
Celia Knight, the designer was Elliot Epstein, and the
production supervisor was Teresa F. Leaden. It was set in
Melior by J. M. Post Graphics, Corp.

Printed and bound by The Book Press.

To Linda, Herb, Franklin, and
Arthur, and to Harry Rosenbaum,
who always knew what motivated
working people

About the Author

BERNARD L. ROSENBAUM, Ed.D., is president of MOHR Development Inc. in Stamford, Connecticut—the foremost and largest firm designing and developing custom-made behavior modeling training programs. He specializes in the application of behavior sciences to a broad range of interpersonal skills—including management and supervision, sales management, selling, negotiating, interviewing, and more—for a variety of client companies representing such industries as manufacturing, retailing, pharmaceuticals, and banking. Dr. Rosenbaum received his master's and doctorate degrees in industrial psychology from Columbia University. He is a member of the American Psychological Association and is a New York State certified psychologist. He is also president of Personnel Sciences Center in New York City, serving industry in the areas of personnel selection, employee attitude measurement, and career counseling.

Contents

Preface

There is a widening gap between traditional supervisory techniques and worker productivity. Today's work force exhibits less tolerance for authoritarianism, organizational restraints, and dehumanizing work. As a result, traditional leadership styles have become increasingly unresponsive to the needs of today's workers.

Supervisors have been subjected to over two decades of theory and philosophy on the value of participative management, supportive relationships, and humanistic treatment of employees. The average supervisor is more ready than ever to adjust personal style to reflect contemporary social change. For that reason, books written simply to change supervisors' attitudes are no longer as necessary as in the past. Furthermore, such books have had minimal impact on behavior change.

This book focuses on showing supervisors precisely how to implement principles of participative management, how to communicate better, and how to motivate, teach, and lead in the 1980s. The book emphasizes involvement through specific skills-building exercises rather than passively reading. General principles of motivation are presented and provide the organizing concepts and rationales that underlie the learning. The general principles represent the rationale against which modeled behaviors and strategies are built. Models for dealing with the poor performer, the average performer, and the dissatisfied employee are presented with specific action steps to aid the learner in the mastery of the mediating principles. Models are also presented for effectively dealing with disciplinary action, resistance to change, and conflict between employees.

This book teaches an effective but demanding approach to

the management of people. The reader develops skill in maintaining a maximum concern for people while never compromising on productivity. If you are involved in the management of others, you should no longer have to rely on improvisation. You will now have a "flight plan" to help ensure a safe, efficient, and satisfying trip.

Bernard L. Rosenbaum

PART ONE
INTRODUCTION TO MOTIVATIONAL THEORY

There has been a growing recognition on the parts of managers and supervisors in all industries that motivational techniques that were once effective have lost much of their impact. A major segment of our worker population now brings a different set of values and expectations to the job, and there is a widening gap between traditional supervisory techniques and worker productivity. Some of the historical perspectives of the changing needs of the work force will be discussed in Chapter 1, as will the impact of changing needs on worker motivation. Chapter 2 will help to provide a basic knowledge of motivational theory in order to enrich the reader's historical perspective of the changing work force and to provide a rationale for the managerial and supervisory skills discussed in the remainder of the book.

1
BACKGROUND

In Charles Dickens's novel *Hard Times*, a story about life in nineteenth-century industrial England, there is a character named Mr. Bounderby who owns a large mill in a grimy, monotonous little city somewhere in the Midlands. Conditions in Mr. Bounderby's mill are superlatively awful. The work is tedious and dehumanizing, the salaries are abysmal, and the physical environment is filthy and unhealthy. And Mr. Bounderby is understandably defensive about it:

> Now, you have heard a lot of talk about the work in our mills, no doubt. You have? Very good. I'll state the fact of it to you. It's the pleasantest work there is, and it's the lightest work there is, and it's the best-paid work there is. More than that, we couldn't improve the mills themselves, unless we laid down Turkey carpets on the floors. Which we're not a-going to do.

Bounderby is also given to making pronouncements about the needs and ambitions of the mill workers:

> There's not a Hand in this town, Sir, man, woman or child, but has one ultimate object in life. That object is, to be fed on turtle soup and venison with a gold spoon. Now they're not a-going— none of 'em—ever to be fed on turtle soup and venison with a gold spoon.

This, comments Dickens, was always regarded by Mr. Bounderby as "the sole, immediate, and direct object of any Hand who was not entirely satisfied."

HISTORICAL PERSPECTIVES

Under the circumstances, Bounderby's assessment of his "Hands" is ludicrous at best. Battered by long hours, low pay, and dangerous working conditions, they have just begun to agitate for the satisfaction of what today we take for granted as the most basic of human needs. The world of Turkish carpets and gold spoons is not even imaginable to them. They have enough to worry about simply in their desire to be decently fed and clothed, to live and work in a sanitary environment, and to enjoy some measure of job security. But Bounderby is right about this much, at least: his workers' dissatisfaction, and the objectives they are pursuing, can be largely summed up in physical and economic terms. He obviously approaches the problem of job dissatisfaction from a point of view very different from theirs, but the terms are essentially the same. There is comparatively little talk on either side about such modern concerns as job enrichment and self-actualization. (Such concerns are closely in the background, but neither party can really articulate them.) Instead, debate centers on how light or rigorous the work is, how well- or ill-paid the workers are, and whether the mills themselves could be improved. It is the legacy that has characterized management-union struggles right up to our own day: the assumption on both sides that job satisfaction hinges on the proper adjustment of such variables as money and safety, with the only point at issue being how much improvement in those areas is needed.

This nineteenth-century mill owner and his workers share another assumption as well. Whatever economic improvement accrues to the workers, or is withheld from them, is ultimately his responsibility. The most thoughtful of them show no ambition at all for participative management, or formal profit sharing arrangements, or anything of the sort. The relationship is understood by both parties to be essentially a paternal one, and what Bounderby is faulted for is simply a failure to act his paternal role more conscientiously. As Dicken's main working-class character in the novel, Stephen Blackpool, says, it is not for the likes of him and his fellow workers to come up with answers to all their problems. " 'Tis them as is put over me, and over all the rest of us. What do they take upon themselves, Sir, if not to do it?"

RESPONDING TO EMPLOYEE NEEDS

The implications of all this with respect to our present topic, employee motivation, are clear. Bounderby is seen as inspiring rebelliousness among his employees because—to oversimplify for the sake of making the point—he doesn't give them enough. The "win-lose" adversary mentality that he has adopted in the face of their demands has only nourished the same sort of attitudes in them and encouraged them to try to wrench from him the benefits that he will not dispense willingly. On the other hand (it is suggested), if only he had improved their economic condition and their working environment sufficiently, as a good father does for his children, he could have expected loyalty and attention to duty in return. Not a very sophisticated conception of employee motivation on Dickens's part, perhaps, but it could hardly have been otherwise. In comparison to our work force today, the industrial work force in Dickens's age was grossly undereducated, desperately poor, ingrained from earliest childhood with doctrines of submissiveness to authority, and far too enslaved by immediate physical and security needs to worry much about what would happen after those needs had been met. At the time, a benevolent-parent model for management was no more than appropriate.

The work force of the 1970s—and the motivational techniques needed in the 1970s—present a radically different picture; times have changed. Nowhere is this difference more striking than in the area of workers' purchasing power and economic status. To be sure, the modern blue-collar worker's life is still not the life of turtle soup and gold spoons (though a loom operator from Bounderby's mill would probably be too awestruck by modern affluence to notice the difference). The modern pipe fitter or shipping clerk may not feel wealthy but at least does not have to worry about the prospect of starvation-level poverty, or being forced to live in disease-ridden slums, or being unable to find the minimal amount of warm clothing needed to protect the family in winter. A glance back at Dickens's era is a useful reminder of just how far we have come in the last century: the advances that social reformers, labor union movements, and the mass production of consumer goods have brought about in workers' abilities to satisfy the basic human needs—and more—have been little short of enormous. And the affluence of the white-collar professional has increased proportionately.

HIERARCHY OF NEEDS

The fact that these economic changes in the work force have taken place is obvious; the question is "What do they mean for those whose business it is to motivate others in the work force?" In *Motivation and Personality* (1954) psychologist Abraham H. Maslow published a theory of human motivation centering on a so-called hierarchy of needs, a term which has by now become part of the standard vocabulary of behavioral scientists and students of business administration.

At the bottom of Maslow's hierarchy are the physiological needs (food, water, warmth, sex, and so forth), followed at the next level by "safety" or security needs (which include both literal physical safety and the feeling of being protected against future injury or financial hardship). When these needs are fulfilled, and only then, the motivational effects of the higher-order needs come into play. Those higher-order needs—love and belonging, esteem, and (at the top of the hierarchy) "self-actualization"—we can return to in the next chapter. What is of interest here are the physiological concerns and the concerns with security: the concerns, in other words, of Bounderby's workers. If Maslow was right (and there has been a considerable amount of research backing him up), modern affluence has radically reduced the power of those concerns as motivators: "a satisfied need is no longer a motivator of behavior." Behavioral experts have recognized for some time now that a concentration on economic and security incentives can produce only limited gains in worker productivity. The manager who seeks to motivate employees simply by giving them more in the way of physical and economic benefits is following a method that has long since passed a point of diminishing returns.

DIFFERENT MOTIVATORS FOR TODAY'S WORKERS

None of this is to say, of course, that physical and economic well-being are not still necessary ingredients in job satisfaction; they are. Nor would anyone claim that employees cannot be motivated by the hope of merit raises or promotions accompanied by higher salaries; obviously they can. But research indicates that, for the long term, the most you can do by satisfying the lower-order needs and nothing else is to produce a *neutral* attitude toward the job. And it has become clear from the large numbers of dissatisfied workers in the 1970s, particularly among the young, that you often can't do even that. As for the motivation supplied by the prospect of raises or promotions, we are clearly dealing here with a pursuit of money that is in most cases *symbolic* of a pursuit of other kinds of self-fulfillment: status, for example, or the ability to buy things that bring status. This is a type of motivation that may have some effect on the behavior of individuals but can have very little on the behavior of groups, because if everyone in a group gets a raise, no one's individual status in the group is enhanced. And even in the case of the employee who is rewarded as an individual, what happens when you reach a point where further promotion is no longer possible, or where the employee already has a swimming pool in the backyard and the kids safely through college? Everybody likes money. But nowadays the status it produces—or the "esteem," to use Maslow's better concept— plainly needs to be sought in other ways as well.

Increased affluence is not, however, the only significant difference between today's work force and yesterday's. Observers have also reported striking changes, even within the past 20 years or so, in the degree to which workers are willing to rely on authority figures and to accept authoritarian styles of management. Part of the reason is simply that the average workers of the 1970s have had far more formal education than their predecessors. Especially among young men and women in the

20- to 34-year age group—where the largest increases in worker population have been occurring—it is not at all uncommon nowadays to find educational histories that include 1, 2, and even 3 or more years of college experience. A background in higher education is no longer the exclusive property of professional employees and top management. This doesn't necessarily mean that modern workers are any smarter than their parents or grandparents. (How many of us really are?) It does mean that their *perceptions* of themselves have changed and that they are much less likely to put up with a supervisory style of treating them as if they were ignorant.

This change has been buttressed by the increasing permissiveness in our schools and our child rearing practices in general. Whether one regards the new permissiveness as "good" or "bad," it is a fact of our times. Young men and women who are the products of our public schools over the last few years, for example, have almost certainly never had their knuckles rapped or their bottoms caned for their failure to do an assignment. And, especially if they've gone on to college, they've probably been exposed to an atmosphere in which value is placed on debate, discussion, questioning, and exploration. New employees with that kind of background are far more likely than their forebears to ask *why* an assigned task has to be performed, or why it has to be performed in one certain way and no other. What happens if the supervisor of such an employee, to take an example, replies to the question by snarling, "Because I say so. You just do your job, and leave the whys to me"? Obviously the employee has a problem—and so does the supervisor, with any desire at all to motivate the employee. Condescension won't work; the "strong, silent" approach won't work; and the verbal bottom beating certainly won't work. Taken as a whole, the work force today is simply not as prone to let itself be "whipped into line" as it used to be.

Besides, the growth of the communications media, especially television, has altered the role of even the benevolent authority figure. When I was a child during World War II, I remember, my father would bring home *The New York Times* every evening and, with the help of maps, explain the troop movements and the progress of the battles to me. That, and that alone, was the way I got my information about what was happening in the war. I depended on him completely and accepted his every explanation as if it had been handed down verbatim from the mouth of God. Nowadays, of course, my own kids have instant access to news from the other side of the world simply by flicking on the tube. I am still an authority for them, but they have networks full of other authority figures as well—together with the illusion that they are forming their own judgments of the facts, without any bias by an authority figure at all. They do not depend on so *narrow* and *local* a set of authority figures as my generation did. The same will be true of their attitudes toward their supervisors when they enter the work force. The first supervisor will indeed be an authority figure for them, but having seen the way other leaders from around the world act (at least in public), they will be less inclined to accept the behavior of this one supervisor as a definition of the way all bosses behave. Simultaneously, by opening up the broader world to them, television will have increased their perception of the variety of career options available to them. They will feel that they don't *need* the approval of some particular supervisor in some particular place as much as their father did. They can always do something else.

Add to all this the increased mobility of the modern employee, the power of the modern labor union, and the impact of modern EEOC (Equal Employment Opportunity Commission) regulations, and the picture begins to come into focus: employees' perceptions of their roles vis-à-vis management are changing, and traditional leadership styles are becoming more and more irrelevant—even counterproductive. The danger for the present-day manager does not lie simply in Bounderby-style bullying. Every experienced manager knows what kinds of reactions that can elicit: hostility, rebelliousness, in some cases downright subversion. These are easily recognized problems. But the more common and insidious type of employee problem is apathy, unresponsiveness, a merely pro forma performance of duties. And for this, according to the research, we can blame the kind of paternalism recommended by Dickens as much as the kinds of threats uttered by Bounderby. There is a great deal of evidence to suggest that some of the things the workers of the 1970s have most wanted (and have been most motivated by when they have had them) are autonomy, responsibility, independence—or, at a minimum, a leadership style that implicitly recognizes the worker's *capacity* for autonomy and responsibility. The manager confronted with a behavioral problem that seems to stem from some vague dissatisfaction on the employee's part would not expect to resolve it simply with a tongue-lashing, and it has become increasingly clear that the manager can no longer count on resolving it by being "generous" or "kind" either. The old paternalistic styles cannot be relied on the way they once were.

To some extent, of course, the challenges posed by the changing needs of employees can be dealt with (and in due course must be dealt with) by changes in organization design. Job enrichment programs, the opening of horizontal as well as vertical lines of communication, the inclusion of workers in team problem-solving efforts, a decreased reliance on old authority-centered evaluation procedures—in a host of ways, organizational structures are beginning to respond to the altered need-structures of the work force. But responses on such a large scale come about slowly, as everyone knows. The vast majority of managers with supervisory responsibilities still operate in fundamentally traditional organizations and will probably continue to do so at least in the immediate future. Moreover, no amount of organizational rearrangement, and no amount of redefinition of the supervisor's role, is ever going to free the supervisor from the necessity of understanding and coping with the "people problems" that affect job performance. Organizations may design helpful new *formats* for coping with such problems, but a format isn't the same thing as a solution. Supervisors will still find themselves on the front lines—with people firing incomprehensible new weapons at them—and will still have to come up with new ways of surviving with honor.

SKILL DEVELOPMENT VERSUS ATTITUDE CHANGE

Fortunately, the typical supervisor of today has also been changing, or at least undergoing preparations for change, to try to
keep up with the challenges of the job. For over a decade now,
behavioral scientists, trainers, and personnel professionals have
been immersing supervisors in programs designed to alter their
approaches to their employees. They have been introduced,
many of them, to new ideas about such things as the basic
nature of human beings and their needs, the correlates and
determinants of job satisfaction, and the characteristics of the
effective leader. They have heard about up-to-date theories on
the values of participative management, supportive relationships, and a humanistic treatment of employees. They have had
their consciousness raised by group sessions focusing on human relations, sensitivity training, and transactional analysis.
And as a result of all this there has been, on the whole, a growth
in their general awareness of the importance of the "people
components" of management. Whether that awareness really
reflects any deep or lasting attitudinal change is another question. But it can be said that their training experiences have
made them—again, on the whole—more receptive to new management concepts and more ready to adapt their style to reflect
contemporary social change.

So far so good. The trouble is, most supervisors still don't
know *how* to put their increased awareness to work. There is
some evidence that training programs can have an impact on
the trainee's attitudes; there is a good deal more that they can
increase the trainee's intellectual insights into the personality
development and motivational structure of employees. But thus
far, research has produced generally disappointing answers as
to the extent to which improved attitudes and intellectual insights affect a supervisor's *on-the-job behavior*. (And, to the
extent to which they do affect behavior, there is not much indication that the new behavior is always productive and motivating.) Of course a few rare managers have so many native
interpersonal skills that all they need is a few concepts to help
them focus what they are already doing. But there are plenty

of other managers around who are more than willing to reshape their interpersonal styles, have participated in half a dozen T group sessions, have come away with a head full of all the right attitudes, and who still don't know how to do things like reduce an employee's resistance to change. They understand perfectly well that they are not dealing with such situations effectively; what they need is not more consciousness raising but help in converting their attitudes and insights into behavioral skills that they will actually find useful on the job. That is what this book is about.

LOOKING AHEAD

In the next chapter we will be looking briefly at some of the more influential modern theories of management, but not for their own sakes. Though supervisory skills training is grounded in theory, it is not primarily concerned with what people think in the abstract. The primary concern is to pick out from the theory the basic principles of effective supervision in today's business world and then to see how those principles can be implemented. Having grasped the general nature of the challenges they have to meet, managers must try to define for themselves the kind of supervisory style that will fill the bill. Then they can turn their attention—as this book does—to specific ways of putting that style into action. That is our ultimate goal: changing supervisory behavior so that it affects the real-world performance of today's employees. A reminder of some of the trends in current theory and research is a necessary start—but only a start—toward that goal.

2

REVIEW OF
MOTIVATIONAL THEORY

Although the focus of this book is on the practical and everyday rather than on the theoretical, a basic knowledge of motivational theory may be of interest to those who wish to know more about the origins of the motivational skills to be discussed. This chapter does not propose to be an exhaustive review of the literature in the field; rather, it is designed to isolate those concepts which have the most relevance for managers and supervisors who are interested in creating more motivating work environments. The remainder of the book will place these concepts into real life contexts and apply them to specific situations.

THE MANAGERIAL GRID ®

One of the most influential tools in the evolution of behavior modeling is the Managerial Grid. Developed by Drs. Robert R. Blake and Jane S. Mouton, the Grid has been widely used since the early 1960s as a model for organization development interventions. The thesis of Blake and Mouton is that the conventional polarization managers tend to make between a concern for people and a concern for production is counterproductive: the successful manager is one who knows how to integrate employee needs with production needs and capitalize on both. The Managerial Grid attempts to move beyond the vagueness of that technique by providing a graphic illustration, or paradigm, of managerial styles based on two variables: concern for human beings and concern for production. At one extreme is the manager who exhibits neither caring for people nor interest in production; at the other is the manager who is entirely committed to both. (See Exhibit 1.) The five

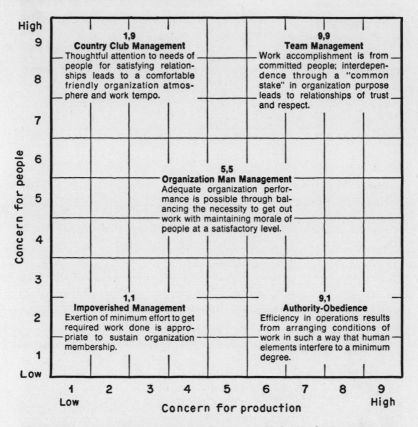

EXHIBIT 1 **The Managerial Grid®** (*From Blake and Mouton, 1978, p. 11. Reproduced by permission.*)

fundamental managerial styles on the Grid may be summarized as follows.

The manager who is 9,1-oriented is autocratic and authoritarian, an old-line "boss" whose main concern is with status and rank, whose energies go into dominating others and solidifying authority, who suppresses conflict and maintains a "produce or perish" ethic. The sensitivity of such a manager to human needs and interactions is virtually nonexistent.

Type 1,9 is the radical opposite of 9,1 and is labeled by Blake and Mouton as "country club management." While the managers in this category do concern themselves with a cheerful and harmonious work force—with all the requisite picnics and company recreations—they do so at the expense of production. Workers behave like contented cows but produce little. The work atmosphere is so single-mindedly relaxed and laid back that all conflicts are smoothed over, all bad news played down.

More abysmal yet is category 1,1, or "impoverished management." This style is characterized by impotent leadership on all levels: the manager has little concern for production or people and functions only on a survival level; the whole point of being in business is to put in time, avoid tough issues, and wait for retirement.

Between these extremes is 5,5, or "middle-of-the-road" management. The manager in this category maintains a steady compromise between caring about employees and caring about business, so much so that the company has a pervasive blandness and mediocrity. The manager performs adequately in both areas, maintaining a "firm but fair" consistency, and never sets his or her sights very high.

The 9,9 manager, on the other hand, insists on excellence in both areas by integrating a maximum sensitivity to people with a maximum concern for production. The two concerns are viewed as utterly interdependent, with the underlying assumption that "people support what they help create." The manager who opts for this style of "team management" does not abdicate authority but acts as a coach, adviser, and consultant who communicates feelings and facts to employees in order to work out creative solutions to problems.

Although the Grid is designed to aid supervisors in defining their own style of supervision, the ultimate goal is to produce 9,9 managers. As we shall see, supervisory skills training (SST) goes a step beyond this goal by providing concrete illustrations of how 9,9 managers utilize this style in *specific* situations. Our concern in a modeling approach is not merely with making managers aware of the superiority of team management skills but with providing concrete examples, having the manager practice the skills, reinforcing the newly learned behavior, asking the manager to make a commitment to practicing this style in the job setting, and, again, positively reinforcing the manager for doing so.

THEORY X AND THEORY Y

Traditionally, whatever style a manager has chosen has been dependent upon the manager's view of people in general. One of the first theoreticians to challenge managers to look at these assumptions was Douglas McGregor (1960), a professor of industrial management at M.I.T. who became convinced that management must base its practices on the insights of behavioral science if it is to be a real profession. McGregor's contribution was to divide managerial attitudes toward employees into two divisions, each of which presupposes a basic philosophy of human behavior. He called these two views of people in relation to work Theory X and Theory Y.

Theory X is the conventional view of humans engaged in the work situation. According to this view, the average person has an intrinsic aversion to work and will avoid it if possible. The manager must therefore exercise coercion, control, and the threat of punishment to harass workers into even mediocre effort. Indeed, the average person prefers to be controlled and directed: an individual on the job has relatively little ambition and desires security above all. Theory X thus implies that people are lazy, dull-witted, uncooperative, and greedy. The supervisory style which flows from these assumptions includes rigid controls, the use of punishment as a motivator, and an exclusive reliance on monetary rewards. Since people generally live up to expectations, employees who are treated as slovenly, incompetent, and unambitious often behave that way.

Radically opposed to this traditional management philosophy is Theory Y, a construct formulated by McGregor based on behavioral science. Theory Y is the inversion of Theory X: if workers are lazy and lackadaisical, it is not because they are inherently that way but because management creates their ennui through excessive control. According to Theory Y, the expenditure of both physical and mental effort in work is as natural as play or rest. The average person has an inherent need to be self-motivated and self-controlled, and the shrewd manager is one who knows how to recognize and tap that need so that a worker can learn to accept and seek responsibility. In an environment oriented toward personal and organizational growth—one which recognizes human imagination and problem-solving ability—individual needs are (as we have seen on the Managerial Grid) consonant with company goals. McGregor emphasized that the contrasting managerial styles implicit in Theory X and Theory Y represent not differences in degree but fundamentally different visions of life. He also stressed that a truly participatory environment, one based on Theory Y, is nonmanipulative: manipulation is the atmosphere of providing an illusion of participation, not real choice or influence. McGregor prefers honest coercion to manipulation. The manager who manipulates is not only someone with a "lack of integrity" but someone who has little pragmatic sense: once workers recognize that they are being manipulated, they strike back by devising ingenious ways to defeat managerial purposes.

Douglas McGregor was clearly not the stereotype of the cold behavioral scientist but a person who proposed an optimistic and humanistic view of human beings at work, one which maximizes self-motivation and minimizes external control. It is this view, McGregor's Theory Y, which provides a key part of the foundation for the SST process.

HIERARCHY OF NEEDS

In the background of McGregor's Theory Y is the work of another influential behavioral scientist, Abraham H. Maslow. Maslow's research influenced not only McGregor's Theory Y but a large part of the behavioral science movement in industry. Ironically, until after 1962 Maslow seemed largely unaware of the relevance of his research to the world of work, even though he formulated a systematic theory of motivation which has had a profound impact on that world.

Maslow called this now well-known theory the "hierarchy of needs." Based on the assumption that motivation comes from within and cannot be imposed, the hierarchy of needs advances three basic propositions:

1. Since human beings are wanting animals, human behavior is determined by unsatisfied needs; a satisfied need no longer motivates behavior.

2. Human needs exist in a hierarchy of importance.

3. Higher needs differ from lower needs in that they are never completely satisfied.

Graphically, Maslow's hierarchy of needs is shown in Exhibit 2.

Human needs are listed on the chart beginning with the most primitive and ranging upward to the most utopian. The physical level involves a need for such primary things as food, water, shelter, and sex. When these fundamental needs are not met, no other higher-level needs will act as motivators. On the other hand, once primary needs are satisfied, safety or security needs are activated. These include protection from physical harm,

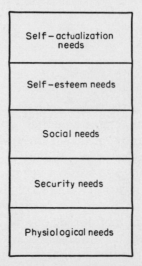

EXHIBIT 2   Hierarchy of needs. (*After Maslow, 1970.*)

sickness, and economic disaster and "futuristic" needs in that they represent a desire to ensure an ability to satisfy physical needs. The next level up is the social level, the need for belongingness and love. This can come into play only when physical and safety needs are reasonably secured. Related but on a higher level is the need for esteem, self-respect, and a feeling of competency. Esteem needs are divided into two categories: the need for experiencing a personal worth and competency, and the need for recognition and admiration in the eyes of others. Less easy to define is the highest level, self-actualization, the process of making actual the person's perception of his or her real self. A rarely attained (or even sought after) state, self-actualization is the impulse to become what one is capable of becoming, of achieving one's full potential in the most creative, self-motivated way.

The upper levels of Maslow's hierarchy are an attempt to explain why people continue to strive for excellence even when lower-level needs have been met. It is a dynamic model which posits multiple needs operating simultaneously. For our purposes, the higher-level needs are most crucial: assuming that the physical, safety, and social needs of the employee are being reasonably fulfilled, the behaviors in this book offer the supervisor techniques to enhance workers' self-esteem and confidence and thus enhance performance.

COGNITIVE DISSONANCE

Another concept which has moved managers toward recognizing the importance of workers' self-esteem is the theory of cognitive dissonance (Festinger, 1957). Simply stated, this theory—which may at first seem irrelevant to business concerns—posits that conflict occurs when beliefs or assumptions are contradicted by new information. This conflict produces feelings of discomfort which the individual may attempt to assuage by actually reconciling the differences, by convincing himself or herself that they do not exist, or by generating various defense mechanisms. If, for example, a supervisor's management style results in poor worker motivation, the manager might move to adopt a different style or might instead choose to ignore the evidence or demand more of it. In other words, cognitive dissonance explains the common human tendency to screen out unpleasant data. There appears to be a desire for consistency, or consonance, in human behavior and a need to make inconsistent ("dissonant") experiences consonant.

The immediate relevance of this theory to business is that if workers have negative perceptions about themselves, they need negative outcomes to achieve the consistent result. Work climates which focus on incompetence inspire incompetent performances, just as work climates which focus on self-competency inspire competent performances.

SELF-IMPLEMENTATION

An important elaboration of this theory is provided by Abraham Korman (1971) in his standard text, *Industrial and Organizational Psychology*. Calling his theory "self-implementation," Korman asserts that the higher a worker's perception of personal competence is, the more effective will be the performance. Supervisors capable of creating environments conducive to self-confidence increase the chances of getting competent performance. Nothing succeeds like success; nothing fails like failure. In addition, Korman points out different kinds of perceived self-competency:

Chronic: The persistent opinion one has of oneself; a generalized feeling regarding the level of competency

Situational: The opinion one has of oneself based upon a situation; a feeling regarding competency in handling certain kinds of tasks

Socially defined: A feeling of competency based upon the given social contexts of the moment

The models we present in this book do not attempt to change individuals with chronically low perceptions of their own competency. Instead, our techniques are most effective as initial interventions which help prevent chronic poor performance from developing in the first place.

TWO-FACTOR THEORY

In this context, the motivation theories of Frederick Herzberg (1966) are of special interest, for Herzberg addresses himself to those elements in the workplace which produce worker satisfaction and dissatisfaction. According to Herzberg, they flow from entirely different factors, and the failure of management to motivate workers in the past can be attributed to a larger failure to see the distinction.

Herzberg uses the term "hygiene factors" to isolate aspects of a job which prevent or promote dissatisfaction but do not yield satisfaction. These include company policy, pay, job security, and working conditions. As an example, Herzberg cites fringe benefits: workers grumble if they don't have benefits, but the existence of benefits does not in itself produce motivation.

Factors that do produce motivation include achievement, recognition, advancement, responsibility, and interesting work. Achievement includes the successful completion of a job, finding solutions to problems, and seeing the results of one's work; recognition is a feeling of personal accomplishment with a completed task; advancement refers to promotion; responsibility is a worker's control over his or her job, including the ability to perform without supervision; and interesting work includes variety as opposed to routine, creativity as opposed to stultification, and challenge as opposed to repetitiveness. The last category is especially important, for it concerns the actual content of the job and its impact on the employee: whether a person spends 8 hours of a day feeling bored or feeling worthwhile is surely a fundamental factor in determining motivation.

Part of the inspiration for Herzberg's theory clearly comes from Maslow and his hierarchy of needs: Herzberg's "motivators"—those factors which give the employee a sense of pride and accomplishment—correspond with Maslow's "higher" needs, while the hygiene factors are equivalent to Maslow's lower-order needs for safety and survival. Thus the hygiene factors are important and must be adequately provided if the person is to transcend them and experience higher levels of "motivation" and "self-actualization." Our goal here is to show supervisors how to build "motivators" into job interactions through the actual modeling of behavior designed to meet basic human needs for achievement, responsibility, and self-esteem.

THEORY OF PERSONAL CAUSATION

A useful underpinning of Herzberg's theory is DeCharms's *Personal Causation: The Internal Affective Determinants of Behavior* (1968), which holds that the primary motivation of humans is the need to effectively cause changes in the environment. Most people do not want to have their lives be determined, to be manipulated, to be pawns. People value most highly the behavior that they believe they have originated themselves rather than the behavior they perceive as having been imposed upon them. Students, for example, are more likely to cherish and remember the insights they seize themselves in the process of a class interaction rather than the insights a teacher spoon-feeds them in a lecture. In the same way, a supervisor who encourages employees to originate their own work and who actively listens to and has respect for their ideas is ensuring that the employees will value that work more highly.

TRANSACTIONAL ANALYSIS

Another way to look at the pragmatic value of the SST approach is from the perspective provided by Transactional Analysis (TA), a technique of psychotherapy which has found application in the workplace. Created by Eric Berne in 1957, TA has been popularized through the best-selling books *Games People Play* (Berne, 1964), *I'm OK—You're OK* (Harris, 1973), and *Born to Win* (James and Jongeward, 1971).

TA offers a style of human interaction without coercion. The first step in the TA process is becoming aware that all transactions flow from three states of mind: "Parent," "Adult," and "Child." The parent state is a vast psychological storehouse of teachings and approbations from the past by parent figures; these are recorded in the brain and play out repeatedly in the present, so much so that Berne compares them to old tape recordings which play of their own volition, even when their messages are inaccurate or inappropriate. The adult state, on the other hand, is the part of the personality which can take in new options and act on them in the here and now, without being controlled by tapes from the past. Finally, the child state is defined as a chaos of childhood feelings both from the past ("taped in" like the parent statements) and from the present. Misunderstandings or "crossed transactions" occur when a statement made by a person in one state is encoded in a different state, thereby ending or distorting communication. A frequent type of transaction occurs when a parent statement is made by a supervisor to a subordinate, thus causing the subordinate to react to a reprimanding parent. In the business world, such a transaction usually goes something like this:

SUPERVISOR: You have a poor attitude, and you're always complaining.

EMPLOYEE: You always blame me when something goes wrong.

Since the adult is oriented toward results and is in touch with the here and now, it is usually the most effective ego state for business transactions. A mutual exchange based on mutual trust—what TA lingo refers to as "I'm OK—You're OK"—is an adult style of interaction which builds self-esteem and makes for better business. The more traditional parent-child interaction often favored by management, "I'm OK—You're Not OK," results in a depressing work environment which lowers a worker's self-esteem, generates defensiveness, and subverts good performance.

BEHAVIOR MODIFICATION

Another significant approach to building a productive work environment is provided in the "Operant Conditioning" principles of B. F. Skinner (1938, 1974). Skinner is by far the most controversial theorist covered in the chapter: denounced by everyone from theologians to Marxists, Skinner has become the most visible stereotype of the "cold," "mechanistic," "totalitarian" behavioral scientist. His hard-line determinism—an insistence that all human behavior is determined by external stimuli and that "free will" is an illusion—has been widely condemned as inimical to fundamental Judeo-Christian values and to the very idea of democracy. On the other hand, his concrete proposals for building a more rational environment through the establishment of new contingencies and controls have been cited by his admirers as enlightened and revolutionary contributions to civilization.

Whatever one thinks of Skinner's unyielding determinism, there is no question that operant conditioning has a place in business and industry. Indeed, the idea of "reinforcement" is commonly accepted as an "empirical law of effect," and reinforcement techniques are commonly used by educators and psychologists to change behavior—either to strengthen desirable behavior or to diminish undesirable behavior by rewarding the one and punishing or ignoring the other.

The issue of what constitutes the "appropriate" use of reinforcement in a business environment will be discussed in Chapters 4 and 5. For our final summary of motivational theory as it relates to management, let us note that a focus on behavior rather than on personality increases the chances that employees will understand their problems and goals, feel competent to attain those goals, receive valuable feedback on their progress, and be evaluated objectively rather than in terms of a supervisor's biased expectations. In all these ways, a focus on behavior can be a vital factor in promoting self-esteem and, consequently, effective performance. To put it in Skinnerian terms, "positive reinforcement," the building of self-confidence and competence, is one of our main concerns in this book. As we shall see, an important fact of that building process is learning to actively listen to employees and learning to help them set clear, solid goals.

A reader who is conversant with the "human potential movement" in the business world might well ask at this point why we have not discussed "sensitivity training," especially since it is based on an ideology which aggressively promotes self-esteem and self-actualization. The reason is simply that our approach is radically different: whereas sensitivity training, as its name implies, focuses on making people more sensitive to their behavior and on making people feel good about themselves, behavior modeling translates these good feelings into specific actions and teaches managers to deal with problems.

What we have covered in this chapter does not constitute a complete overview of all the current diverse views on motivating people at work. (To cite only one example, it leaves out of account the current interest in the motivational effects of group activities such as team problem solving and task-force planning.) Even such a brief survey should be enough, however, to suggest that on several fundamental points there is a coherent body of opinion to build on. These points suggest some of the behavior patterns that must today be considered indispensable equipment for any manager-supervisor who wants to motivate people effectively.

CONVERTING THEORY TO BEHAVIOR

If we recast the points we have been discussing in terms of personal supervisory style, there emerges a list of essential behaviors that might be worded something like this:

1. In general, a style of interacting with employees in ways that will maintain and enhance their self-esteem

2. Active listening that shows understanding of and respect for employees' feelings and ideas and that engages the employees themselves in the process of stating their work problems and considering possible tactics for dealing with them

3. Goal setting that challenges employees supportively, providing them with clear, attainable steps to improved performance

4. An approach to present problems and future objectives that focuses on behavior, not personality, and thus increases the chances that the supervisor and the employee will wind up attacking the problem instead of each other

5. An informed use of reinforcement techniques (a) to define the kinds of behavior that will make the em-

ployee successful in the organization, (b) to encourage
the continuation of such behavior until it becomes regular practice, and (c) to maintain ongoing communication between employee and supervisor

Strictly speaking, perhaps, no one of these behaviors is really
"essential." In fact, the most heavy-handed and authoritarian
of supervisors *can* sometimes succeed in motivating employees,
at least for the short run, by sheer force of example, through
fear of punishment, or because of special crisis circumstances.
(At the other extreme, it is possible to find supervisors who are
fuzzy and inept in almost every respect but whose employees
work hard. Again, for the short run, simply because they like
their supervisor too much to let him or her look bad.) But such
styles are scarcely very dependable models. For the leader who
happens not to be extraordinarily charismatic, or lucky, it is
behavioral skills like the ones just listed that research and theory are now pointing to as common denominators of effective
motivation. Together, these skills outline a supervisory style
reflecting guiding principles for manager-employee relations.

Ultimately, however, these behaviors are important not because theory and logical coherence indicate that they *should*
be useful but because, simply, experience in today's work climate has repeatedly shown that they *are* useful. A review of
their theoretical underpinnings helps to explain their value and
organize them in the mind, but what matters is that the behavioral extensions of the theories "work," that time and again, in
countless types of work situations across a wide range of organizations, the presence or absence of these skills emerges as
a fundamental reason why a leader has succeeded or failed. As
we turn now to the heart of our subject, the translation of theory
into action, we will be focusing on these same behaviors,
slightly rearranged for the sake of clarity, and discussing their
practical uses in more detail. They are our central mediating
principles or rationales under which a host of other more specific skills cluster. And in the final section of the book, "Models
for Motivation," we will find them useful again, both as a framework for recommended "action steps" (guidelines for specific

action in specific circumstances) and as points of reference for understanding how the supervisors in various sample situations have handled the situations effectively. A mastery of these behaviors gives the manager a repertoire of solid, concrete methods for dealing with "people problems" that crop up every day in actual job settings.

PART TWO
TRANSFERRING THEORY INTO ACTION
Principles of Supervisory Skills Training (SST)

In the next five chapters we will take the theoretical propositions of Chapter 2 and glean from them five action principles designed to help managers become effective people handlers. Some successful managers employ these five principles of motivation instinctively. Others may agree with them in theory but ignore them in practice. Still others—such as an angry executive who dealt with a careless supplier by barking, "Who's running things there, the Marx Brothers?"—handle people in ways that sabotage the desired result. In any case, the managers who master these five principles and learn to use them consciously can consistently apply them to new and difficult situations, even those in which they have not had specific training. These principles can help a person be a more skillful manager in a variety of contexts; they can be useful in dealing with suppliers, upper management, employees, customers, community leaders, government regulators, and even people in one's personal life.

3

MAINTAINING AND ENHANCING
THE EMPLOYEE'S SELF-ESTEEM

In this chapter we will focus on one of the most important principles of motivation, the value of maintaining and enhancing self-esteem. This principle is so important that it is a thread which runs throughout the SST program. We emphasize it because its impact on job performance has been demonstrated by research time and again.

Stated simply, this principle asserts that people are motivated to work at a level consistent with their perceptions of self-competency. The individual who feels adequate in performing a task will perform, or certainly be highly motivated to perform, in a manner consistent with that feeling. On the other hand, an individual who is programmed to feel mediocre or incompetent in performing a task will probably live up to those low expectations by producing shoddy work. The supervisor who encourages feelings of competency in subordinates increases the motivation to perform competently; the supervisor who subverts subordinates' self-esteem usually gets a poor-quality product.

In other words, the more confident people feel, the better they perform: an employee who *feels* competent is much more likely to perform competently. If the angry executive who castigated the supplier had understood this principle and tried to maintain the supplier's self-esteem and self-confidence, service could have been brought up to a satisfactory level. Instead, the executive's harshness produced a defensive reaction. Quick to defend personal self-esteem, the supplier rationalized that the poor service was solely the buyer's problem.

The supervisor's mistake was focusing on the two or three items in the order that were shipped in error. A more productive alternative would have been to focus on the eighteen or twenty that were exactly as specified and *then* go on to focus on the error and not the supplier.

(REVIEWING) SELF-ESTEEM RESEARCH

Anyone who doubts the importance of this principle need only glance at the vast amount of research on motivation such as the theories we have summarized in Chapter 2. A useful starting place is Maslow's *Motivation and Personality* (1954). As we have seen in Chapter 2, human needs are organized hierarchically: the "lower" ones are physical needs and the needs for safety, belongingness, and love; the "higher" needs are the needs for self-esteem and self-actualization. Central to our concerns is self-esteem, which research has shown to be a fundamental human drive for respect and dignity. Self-esteem does not come into play as a basic drive if the lower needs are not satisfied. But once they *are* satisfied, self-esteem becomes a powerful stimulus for motivation, one that cannot be ignored by anyone who manages people.

Put another way, once needs are satisfied, they no longer motivate; only unsatisfied needs can motivate. Since to a large extent lower-order needs *have*, at least in part, been met in recent management history, they no longer act as powerfully as motivators. We are now at a point where the higher needs have been activated. Self-esteem is finally an issue which must be dealt with by business: it doesn't cost much to address, but since it *has* surfaced, the erosion of it invariably results in defensive, unproductive employee behavior. To be successful in today's business world, a manager must at the very least decrease the chances of defensive reactions on the job.

As Harold Sheppard and Neal Herrick have shown in their provocative book *Where Have All the Robots Gone?*, the availability of self-esteem as a motivator is a recent phenomenon. In 1935, for example, the issue was irrelevant. Then the operative issues were money, security, survival, the very things that were in short supply—the lower needs that were not being satisfied. Recently, however, the distinct improvement in the satisfaction of these survival needs has brought with it the activation of a whole new set of drives. Workers have recently begun to complain not so much about a lack of money as about a lack of dignity and respect. As Robert Ardrey has forcefully put it, "the hungry psyche has replaced the hungry belly." With turnover rates, absenteeism, and other forms of alienation and dissatisfaction on the increase even among reasonably affluent workers, managers can no longer afford to maintain the cynical notion that all workers care about is pay. Precisely because most of their basic needs are being met, today's workers do not automatically accept authoritarian, dehumanizing styles of management.

Worker priorities have changed. Statistics show that such benefits as interesting work, sufficient help and equipment to get the job done, sufficient information to get the job done, and enough authority and independence of action to do their jobs are as important to workers as good pay. Indeed, since sufficient pay is often given, they are more important. None of these newly demanded features is a tangible economic benefit. Rather, each of them is either a subtle or direct manifestation of the need for self-esteem. Thus, in using extensive research to answer the question of what really matters to contemporary workers, Sheppard and Herrick come up with something quite different from the traditional "good pay": "It is significant that the two work features which have the most to do with job satisfaction are part of the job content; the work itself: being given a chance to do the things one does best, and whether or not the work is interesting."

The point of the first feature is that managers must instill a sense of confidence and competence—not because making workers feel good is nice but because it is necessary. High turnover rates, mediocre performance, chronic absenteeism, and other symptoms of work malaise are not good business. The manager who makes effective use of the self-enhancement skills developed in this book can minimize these symptoms by getting directly at the sickness: the erosion of self-esteem which characterizes a depressingly large number of manager-employee interactions.

This does not mean that the manager who masters these skills must drastically overhaul his or her personality. We are not insisting, for example, that all managers conform absolutely to the 9,9 "team management" style on the Managerial Grid, even though we highly recommend that style as an exceptionally productive one. (See Chapter 2.) Our approach is situational: there may be times when a resolutely authoritarian 9,1 approach is necessary to meet a crisis; there may even be times when a passive 1,1 approach is appropriate. We have no quarrel with your personal style, whatever it is. No one mode of behavior is appropriate for all situations. Indeed, a *wide* array of behaviors to meet varying situations is best. What we are saying is that the team management style—a style based on the encouragement of debate, experimentation, self-determination, and direct communication—raises the dignity and self-esteem of workers and thus motivates them to do a better job. Team management is a tool well worth adding to one's repertoire.

In learning how to reinforce the self-confidence of employees, the important thing to remember is that people are motivated to work at a level consistent with their perceptions of self-competency toward a given task. This correspondence between self-perception and performance is a consequence of cognitive dissonance, the theory outlined in Chapter 2 which states that people seek consistency in their cognitions and adjust their level of competency in a manner which will ensure such consistency. Thus, if workers have a negative cognition about their ability to perform a task, the result is likely to be negative. Put another way, if managers continually tell workers that they are incompetent, the workers are likely to live up to that expectation.

The implications of this theory (sometimes called "self-implementation") are exceedingly important for the supervisor. If the supervisor encourages feelings of competency in task areas, as well as general feelings of competency in subordinates, the motivation to perform the specific task and the overall job well will be increased. Workers are like everyone else: they behave in tune with their self-perceptions. The more competent people feel, the more competently they perform; the more incompetent they feel, the more incompetently they perform.

Furthermore, according to the findings reported in Abraham Korman's standard text, *Industrial and Organizational Psychology* (1971):

1. Individuals who are told they are incompetent to achieve a specific goal or task, even though they have had no previous experience with the task, will perform worse than those who are told they are competent to achieve the task goals.

2. Self-perceived ability based on previous performance is positively related to later performance.

3. The more a person has failed in the past, the less he or she will aspire to in the future.

4. Groups that have failed previously set their goals in ways that increase the probability of their failing again.

5. Individuals and groups of low self-esteem are less likely to achieve difficult goals they have set for themselves than individuals of high self-esteem.

Given these extensive, carefully documented findings, it is a crime that so many managers habitually undermine their employees' self-images and make those they manage feel incompetent and thus all the more likely to perform incompetently. The popular stereotype of "the boss"—someone who is grumpy, negative, punitive, complaining, and thoroughly demoralizing—often has a depressing accuracy. We do seem to hear from the boss most often when something goes wrong, even though research indicates that we would be far more motivated to do excellent work if our employer would interact with us at least as frequently when things go right.

An interesting variation on the theme of promoting self-esteem has been provided by J. Sterling Livingston of the Harvard Business School in his article "Pygmalion in Management." As an analogy to the impact a manager can have on the behavior of his or her employees, Livingston cites a scene from George Bernard Shaw's *Pygmalion* (1912, 1975) in which Eliza Doolittle explains:

> You see, really and truly, apart from the things anyone can pick up (the dressing and the proper way of speaking, and so on), the difference between a lady and a flower girl is not how she behaves, but how she's treated. I shall always be a flower girl to Professor Higgins, because he always treats me as a flower girl, and always will; but I know I can be a lady to you, because you always treat me as a lady, and always will.

According to Livingston, the majority of managers are like Professor Higgins: they unintentionally treat their workers in a manner which leads to a lower level of performance than what they are capable of achieving.

The generalization we can draw from this "Pygmalion effect" is that if a manager's expectations are high, productivity is likely to be superior, but if they are low, productivity is likely to be inferior. Stated positively, a successful manager is one who has the ability to create high performance expectations that subordinates fulfill; stated negatively, an unsuccessful manager is one who fails to instill positive expectations and who thereby sets up a situation in which performance suffers. The implications for workers are simple enough: workers tend to do what they believe they are expected to do.

We are back to the issue of the self-fulfilling prophecy. The managers of one sales organization treated certain sales personnel as "supersalesmen." These individuals then did what they knew supersalesmen are expected to do. The managers also had salespeople with poor productivity records. These workers were treated by their supervisors as not having any chance of success.

In an attempt to protect what was left of their low self-esteem, these salespeople avoided situations that might lead to greater failure—the very situations that could also lead to success. The dismal results were perfectly predictable.

SOME WAYS TO ENHANCE SELF-ESTEEM

The following is a list of specific ways to inspire motivation and enhance self-esteem. At first glance, some of the ways may seem superficial or trite. Nevertheless, if they are used consistently, the accumulation of them will have a positive impact on motivation.

1. Praise the specific task or job.
2. Give special assignments.
3. Give the "OK" signal when you agree with others.
4. Actively listen.
5. Write down others' ideas.
6. Take ideas seriously.
7. Accept others' opinions.
8. Accept differences in others.
9. Express feelings.
10. Recognize feelings.
11. Give tangible rewards.
12. Recognize important events in others' lives.
13. Document highlights (events).
14. Arrange for the boss to acknowledge good work.
15. Point out the good consequences of another's actions. (Point out the product.)
16. Spend time with others.
17. Support others' actions.
18. Ask for opinions on how to solve problems.
19. Delegate.
20. Ask for help.
21. Share experiences.
22. Admit you are wrong.
23. Say, "You are right."

24. Repeat compliments from others.

25. Say, "Hi! How are you?"

26. Show constructive concern about performance problems.

27. Shake hands.

28. Smile.

29. Ask about others' interests.

30. Invite someone to join you for coffee.

31. Inquire (with empathy) about someone's family problems.

32. Provide a new piece of equipment.

33. Ask a person to lead the whole meeting or part of it.

34. Give a teaching assignment.

35. Use the employees' names.

36. Establish and keep follow-up dates.

37. Share information.

38. Give complete reasons for directions.

SKILL PRACTICE EXERCISE 1
Understanding Self-Esteem

In one study employees were asked to select from a list of statements often used by supervisors those which tend to generate a defensive feeling. Over half the employees were in agreement that as to which ones would be most likely to erode their self-esteem and thereby cause a defensive reaction. Those statements are included in the following exercise.

Place a check mark next to each statement you think the employees selected.

Statements That Tend to Erode Self-Esteem

___ **1.** I don't think you're ready for this job, but give it a try.

___ **2.** You just don't seem to understand.

___ **3.** You should know better than to say that.

___ **4.** What are your ideas on how to prevent that from happening again?

___ **5.** You are 10 percent over the budget.

___ **6.** I thought you would have a greater sense of pride in your work.

___ **7.** Your report was 5 days late.

___ **8.** If you would listen, you would understand.

___ **9.** You can't be serious about that suggestion.

___ **10.** The budget doesn't permit additional help.

___ **11.** Don't you think there's a better way to do it than the way you handled it?

___ **12.** This is the safer way to do it.

___ **13.** I hope you're smart enough to know that.

___ **14.** I'm surprised to hear that from someone with your experience.

___ **15.** What led you to that conclusion?

___ **16.** When you're as experienced as I am, then you will understand.

___ **17.** You answered problem 17 incorrectly.

___ **18.** I really thought you knew more than you do about this.

___ **19.** Your below-average score suggests that you need more practice on this exercise.

___ **20.** I just don't know how you can say that.

Answers

The following statements erode self-esteem: 1, 2, 3, 6, 8, 9, 11, 13, 14, 16, 18, 20.

Commentary on Skill Practice Exercise 1

The statements cited as those which tend to erode self-esteem have been carefully tested. They are not *our* opinion of what constitutes counterproductive feedback but the opinion of actual employees.

It should be emphasized that the impact of these statements applies to any situation and to any level of supervisor-employee interaction. For example, any person, whether a secretary or a high-level executive, who is told "I thought you would have a greater sense of pride in your work" will feel defensive and demeaned. There are important principles of psychology which can be profitably utilized by anyone who supervises people.

Not all the statements which evoke a defensive reaction are obvious. A few deserve special comment.

Number 1, for example, is a subtle example of the self-fulfilling prophecy. An employee whose supervisor says "You are not ready for the job" may well live up to (or down to) that low expectation. A free-lance writer who is told by an editor "Well, go ahead and try the piece, but I'm not convinced you're the right person for it" will probably either write a poor article or simply take the article elsewhere. Instead of putting a person in a new position on a trial basis, it is far more effective from a motivational standpoint to say, "Go ahead with it; I have confidence in you." The actual result can then be evaluated by the supervisor later—as it would be in any case.

Numbers 8 and 16 are both parent-type statements which are likely to elicit a defensive, childlike response. (See the material on "I'm OK—You're OK," Chapter 2.) The employee who receives these statements will hear not a supervisor who needs to get a job done but a reprimanding authority figure. The response is likely to be the response of a child—morose, defensive, and rebellious.

Number 11 deserves singling out as a classic example of manipulation.

The employee who hears this statement will think, "Well, how is the boss going to get me to say what the predetermined 'better way' is?" According to employees, this kind of manipulative statement breeds resentment because the employee knows that it is dishonest and that he or she is being manipulated. A more honest and direct approach is for the employer to say, "I think there's a better way." The employer can then state the way and conclude with "What do you think?"

The final question invites active participation and saves the first statement from being authoritarian.

A more obvious debilitating statement is number 9. Yet a high-level executive who was not getting creative ideas from his employees once asked us, with a straight face, why his use of this statement—after an employee in a meeting finally had the nerve to offer a suggestion—produced a room full of dead silence. Even the eroders of self-esteem which should seem obvious are commonly perpetrated by managers, with predictably negative results.

Of the many alternatives to these nonmotivating statements, number 4 is especially effective. The employer who makes a practice of asking workers what their *own* ideas are to prevent something undesirable from occurring again is automatically facilitating problem solving. In this kind of creative interaction, employees feel they have a real ownership in the outcome and therefore are more likely to commit themselves to seeking a solution to the problem.

SKILL PRACTICE EXERCISE 2
Maintaining Self-Esteem

For each of the following supervisor-employee interactions, indicate *(a)* why the statement by the supervisor would have a negative impact on the employee's motivation and *(b)* how the supervisor's statement might be amended in a way that would maintain the employee's self-esteem.

1. *Supervisor:* This code number is wrong! What do I have to do to get you guys to learn?

   a. _____

   b. _____

2. *Supervisor:* What do you think is the best way to deal with the cards? If you take the cards and have the secretaries sign them, then bring them back to me to take to the office, we'll have a smooth system. Do you agree?

   a. _____

   b. _____

3. *Employee:* So what I did was, I took my idea and wrote it up and put it in the suggestion box.
   Supervisor: What idea? What makes you think you know more than other people around here?

   a. _____

   b. _____

4. *Employee:* Hey Joe, why do I have to use these ground wires? It takes forever.

Supervisor: I'm sick and tired of your griping! Would you just do it—it's a company rule.

a. _____

b. _____

5. *Supervisor:* The other day you had an idea, but I was too busy to listen. Now I'm ready to hear it.
Employee: Well, I think it would be good if we required the faculty to turn their grades in the week of the seventh instead of the previous week. That way, we'd have the grades recorded in time to get them back to student advisers before the holidays. . . . Students would then know where they stood and would have time to think about it. . . .
Supervisor: That will never work. Say, can you help me out with the planning chart?

a. _____

b. _____

Answers

1. **a.** Makes employees feel incompetent. Erodes employee's self-esteem.

   b. *Supervisor:* This code number should be changed. The correct number is 10. Be on the lookout for these changes in the future.

2. **a.** Fails to delegate responsibility; discourages a feeling of active participation. Employee feels manipulated.

   b. *Supervisor:* Cathy, I need your help. What's the best way to collect time from the secretaries on the floor?

3. **a.** Makes employee feel incompetent and increases the chances of getting incompetent performance.

   b. *Supervisor:* Thinking of better ways of getting the job done can benefit all of us. Thanks.

4. a. Makes employee feel like a child.

    b. *Supervisor:* Good question, Ron. You see, this stuff is flammable and could start a fire if you don't have those wires.

5. a. Discourages initiative by not acknowledging employee's effort and by not explaining why the idea is unacceptable.

    b. *Supervisor:* I appreciate your thinking of ways to make the system more efficient. Let me explain why I think this particular idea is not likely to work.

4

FOCUSING ON BEHAVIOR, NOT PERSONALITY

Suppose, out of anger, you castigate an unproductive employee by saying "Your work is awful." By saying this, you obviously communicate the message that you are angry, and you probably make yourself feel better by venting your anger. On the other hand, you are violating the basic principle of motivation we discussed in the previous chapter: you are (to put it mildly) eroding the employee's self-esteem and increasing the chances that the employee will become defensive. But the quagmire is deeper than that. By saying "Your work is awful," you are not only saying something that is vague. The employee feels not only demeaned but confused: "*What* work is awful?" the employee wonders. "*Why* is it awful? *What* did I do wrong? Does the boss not like me?" The conversation can only deteriorate from here, and it will probably never address the problem that provoked it in the first place.

DISTINGUISHING BETWEEN PERFORMANCE AND ATTITUDE

Vagueness and how to avoid it are the subjects of this chapter. Vagueness is almost invariably a function of a supervisor's placing the focus on abstractions like the personality and attitude of an employee instead of on the specific behavior which makes the work unsatisfactory.

Suppose the actual source of your anger at your employee was bookkeeping errors. Instead of making a precise blast at how "awful" the work is, you might have simply told the employee that the figures on pages 5, 7, and 12 are wrong and that such errors, if allowed to go unchecked, can cost the company thousands of dollars. A context would then have been established for a discussion of the problem. The bookkeeper would have known precisely what had been done incorrectly and what needed to be corrected.

Sometimes employers are vague even when they think they are making a specific, positive proposal. Suppose, for example, a vice president for sales is conducting a performance appraisal with one of the regional sales managers. In the course of the conversation, the vice president, who believes in being forthright and emphatic in offering suggestions, tells the regional manager to "be more aggressive." Later, the vice president is dismayed to learn that the regional manager has hired two additional district managers. What the vice president had actually meant by "be more aggressive" was that the regional manager's sales goals were 8 percent lower than what they should have been. "Raise your goals by 8 percent" would have been a far better choice of words. It might have lacked the ring of pep-talk oratory, but it would have communicated the message precisely.

Again, the point is to address the problem of performance, not the attitude or personality of the employee. The whole notion of "attitude" is one which merits close attention. "Attitude" is one of the most meaningless and counterproductive jargon words used by managers who think they are inspiring their workers. Unfortunately, it is also one of the most frequently used. One worker is told that she has a "good attitude," another that he has a "bad attitude." What do these appraisals mean? They usually mean only what the worker thinks—or guesses— they mean. Even worse, they can mean what the worker wants them to mean, or what the worker fantasizes the employer means them to mean. Ultimately, the employer who bandies the word "attitude" about with any frequency is setting up a situation in which the employees will never think about their specific behavior—about what they're actually *doing* on the job—because they think the employer is not interested in specifics.

But if the employer is only interested in "attitude," what *is* the employer interested in? Can we *see* a "good attitude," or do we see certain behaviors that cause us to use "good attitude" or "bad attitude" as generalizations? If I hire some writers and am pleased that they always get their copy in on time, will they see why I'm pleased if I praise each one's "attitude" or if I praise each one for making the deadlines?

The problem with an "attitude" is not that it doesn't exist but that it is not directly visible and observable. To say that a person has a "good attitude"—or even a "terrific attitude"—is to make a statement that is indirect and subjective, a statement subject to numerous interpretations. We can't see an attitude because it's at worst an abstraction and at best a vague prediction based on undefined past acts.

We can, however, see behavior. We can observe a worker's actual performance and comment on it directly, in either a positive or negative framework—and we can do this without the slightest reference to the worker's "attitude." To say that we can work only with observable behavior is not to embrace a "behavioristic" philosophy but simply to admit that, at least on the job, we have no other choice. Not only is a worker's general attitude often irrelevant to the specific task at hand; it is invisible. Furthermore, when it *is* relevant, it is decipherable only through observed performance.

"Attitude" is only one of the numerous vague words that cascade out of managers' mouths, to the general confusion of all concerned. Others include "initiative," "hard-working," "mature," "conscientious," and "dedicated." Managers who object that these are perfectly reasonable and clear words should ask themselves a simple question: Do these words tell us what workers are actually *doing* when they manifest these conditions? If they do not, then the employees, even though they may feel good when they hear these kind words, will not have the slightest idea what they are doing to merit the praise.

Equally vague are numerous negative words favored by angry or frustrated managers who give little thought to the impact of their words in relation to how they want their employees to actually behave. Key among these are "lazy," "unambitious," "unreliable," and "uncooperative." Even seemingly straightforward words like "lazy" are actually indirect and subject to many interpretations. The manager who directly tells a worker "You come to work a half hour late" is communicating a much clearer message than the manager who grumbles, "You're lazy."

EXAMPLES OF FOCUSING ON BEHAVIOR

To become more adept at distinguishing vague abstractions from specific performances, let us look at a few more examples. Suppose you tell a worker to "be a good employee." Is there a single behavior or even a commonly agreed-upon group of behaviors which constitutes "being a good employee"? Is "being a good employee" something you can see—or that the worker can see? Is there any other way of telling what this performance is as an alternative to actually seeing it? Because this command is abstract and not concrete, the answer to all these questions is "no." Suppose, on the other hand, you tell an employee to "file a report every Tuesday." Although what constitutes an adequate report many need further clarification, the activity itself is a visible performance. If the worker needs that clarification, there is at least something concrete to talk about. But if you tell the same worker to "feel a sense of commitment" to the work, that worker will be hard put to know what has to be done to convince you that the job has been completed.

In each of these examples, the way to tell whether you are being concrete with a worker is to ask yourself whether your statement refers to a specific single behavior or an observable class of behaviors. Does the statement refer to something you can show the employee? You can show an employee how to set up a new office—but can you show that employee how to "feel a sense of pride in the work"?

Managers who insist on vague communication—who can't resist using jargon such as "maturity," "sense of pride," "attitude," "initiative," and "dedication"—had better define these clichés with some care whenever they use them. If they don't, they are inviting the kind of chaos that invariably results from any massive breakdown in communication. They may, however, be hard put to define any of these words, since the words are all abstract and subjective. In fact, they may be well advised to drop these words from their vocabulary altogether and learn to focus exclusively on outcomes. They may even conclude that they don't care what a worker's "attitude" is—as long as the worker gets the job done.

The real task for the manager is to continually define what constitutes getting the job done. A manager who learns to limit communication to concrete job-related statements—who learns to say "I appreciate your completing this report by 3:00 p.m. on Friday" instead of "I appreciate your cooperation"—no longer needs to get bogged down defining vague generalizations. The mannager can simply eliminate them.

Who needs them really? Apparently, managers think they do, and so, interestingly enough, do teachers and politicians. These three seemingly disparate groups share a common addiction to vague vocabulary. The manager who says "have a positive attitude," the teacher who says "show me some class spirit," and the politician who says "be patriotic" all share an avoidance of specifics, a penchant for vagueness. The politician may know perfectly well the purpose of the statement: the politician may want to avoid specifics, to cloud the issues. But the other two usually think they are clearly communicating their ideas. For them, vagueness can only be unproductive. They don't really want to bewilder their employees and students, to create chaos in the office and classroom, but they somehow think that by using certain buzzwords they are being more "professional"—even though just the opposite is the case.

Many managers even think that sophisticated skills training consists of learning to manipulate employees through clever, indirect language. They labor under the notion that fancy psychological indirection makes for good business, that the more devious and roundabout they are with employees, the easier it is to control them and make them do better jobs. As our examples indicate, nothing could be further from the truth. Employees who are made to feel defensive or bewildered may well be controllable in the short run, but they will hardly be motivated to do a better job, especially if they don't know what doing a better job means. Workers who are labeled "lazy" will simply feel lazy; workers who are told "You come to work late" will feel that they had better start coming on time. Our message to managers is *be straight*—don't be fancy and devious; pinpoint the problem—don't waste your time on indirect personality and attitudinal statements.

Some managers might object at this point that focusing on behavior and performance and not on personality and attitude constitutes "soft management." Shouldn't a manager be tough? Doesn't "toughness" necessitate straightforward statements about the employee's attitude?

Actually, the truth is that managers who see themselves as tough are frequently soft. If we go back to the Managerial Grid discussed in Chapter 2, we see that the 1,9 "country club" management style is characterized by vagueness, by a tendency to be indirect and to play down bad news. Managers who are indirect with employees are not tough at all, but lax: by leaving the specific content of their directives to the imaginations of their workers, they give the workers the leeway to interpret those directives any way they please. A worker typically thinks, "What does the boss mean by 'hard work'? What does the boss mean by 'initiative'? Am I expected to come in on Saturdays? The last person who hired me didn't want me to come in on Saturdays. That boss said that workers who show initiative and work hard are able to finish all their work during the week. . . . I think I won't come in on Saturdays." The soft manager is really the one who used ambiguous language, language which allows employees to adopt any interpretation that fits their needs.

In fact, the direct, no-nonsense method we recommend is actually very demanding. To zero in on the specific problem and forget about "attitudes" is to make the employee take responsibility for his or her actions. If the manager says "Don't come in on Saturdays; complete the task during the week," the message is clear and the worker must take responsibility for doing the job efficiently each day of the week. But the manager who says "work hard" or "take initiative" is encouraging the mental scenario presented in the previous paragraph—hardly a "tough" style of communicating.

NO-NONSENSE METHODOLOGY

The issue of whether to focus on problems or personalities has large reverberations. An inability to focus on specifics can wreak considerable havoc in any work environment. We have already seen how a focus on subjective personality factors instills confusion and defensiveness. Such a focus is dysfunctional for anyone seeking to master communication skills on the job. We have also seen how a subjective emphasis, when used in a negative way, violates the basic principles of motivation outlined in Chapter 3: attacking an unsatisfactory worker's personality is obviously the opposite of enhancing his or her self-esteem. But the problem is larger than that. The issue carries over into the related areas of goal setting, active listening, and positive reinforcement, areas we shall discuss later in this book.

Take goal setting, for example. As we shall see in Chapter 7, a successful manager is one who knows how to maintain communications, set solid goals, and establish specific follow-up dates. But no effective solutions to on-the-job problems can be determined through the maintaining of communication between worker and employer if the problems are not addressed directly in the first place. If a scenario is set up for future discussions of personality—of "attitudes" and "initiative"—the results will be as vague and futile in the future as they are in the present. The real issue will continue to be clouded. Similarly, a manager cannot set challenging but achievable goals for that matter if the issue at hand is an employee's "maturity" or "backbone." Goals can be set only when they refer to concrete tasks.

The issue of clarity also cuts into the use of reinforcement techniques to shape behavior. Reinforcement, as we shall see, encourages desirable behavior and discourages undesirable behavior by the employee's associating a positive response with desirable acts and a negative response or no response with undesirable acts. Positive reinforcement is a particularly potent technique for generating motivation. But a supervisor can't reinforce behavior either positively or negatively if there is no focus on behavior in the first place. There is no way, for example, to positively reinforce a salesperson's "dedication"—a manager can only reinforce an increase in sales. By the same token, there is no way to punish "laziness"—but there are many ways to penalize lateness.

A failure to concentrate on specific problems also under-mines a supervisor's ability to actively listen to employees. As we shall see in Chapter 6, active listening communicates to an employee with a problem the feeling of being understood. It is a crucial component of any interaction which has motivation as a goal. But if the conversation degenerates into an exchange over personality—if the manager snaps, "Oh, you're just a com-plainer"—the worker with the problem will feel the manager is not listening. The worker will also feel, quite rightly, that the problem is being ignored and feelings about the problem are being rejected. Instead of defusing a potentially emotional ex-change and promoting the kind of rapport necessary for solving problems, the manager who emphasizes personality in this way will create a more volatile exchange and make a discussion of the real issues impossible.

Thus, an insistence on using subjective, abstract jargon does wide-ranging damage: it creates a faulty foundation for goal-setting, reinforcement techniques, active listening, and overall behavior mastery. The necessity of emphasizing specific per-formance, instead of personality, is a cornerstone for everything discussed in this book.

But there is one other important area where this issue has an impact: office politics. If a manager is in the habit of spouting vague language and ignoring actual performances, subordinates eventually pick up on this style and use it to their advantage. Where they use it most tellingly is in the politics of promotion. In the slippery, ambiguous atmosphere invariably created by the repeated use of vague language, the question of whether or not to promote an employee revolves not around questions of performance but around questions such as "Is that person a hard worker or a lazy worker?" In such a situation, one contin-gent argues that the person is a hard worker; the other argues that the person isn't. Who is right? Since there is no way to tell—because the question can be interpreted a hundred ways—the issue is usually resolved on the basis of who has the best sales pitch. If certain employees do get a promotion, it is be-cause they were politically savvy enough to stack the deck in their favor, to get the right people to make a pitch for them. In other words, employees are promoted not on the basis of whether or not they have performed well but on the basis of whether or not they are good salespeople. This way increases the chances that incompetent people get promoted to high positions, and the company suffers accordingly.

A COMMUNICATION PITFALL

Managers who wish to avoid the obviously unproductive consequences of such political maneuvering should learn to watch their language—to focus on behavior instead of personality and to promote an atmosphere in which others do the same. In closing, let us study one way to tell the difference between a subjective statement and a concrete statement about behavior. We can ask ourselves a simple question: "Can the task or problem under discussion be seen or observed?" If so, it is a behavior; if not, it is an abstraction. The statement "Jane handles her job with enthusiasm" is an abstraction because her "enthusiasm" is not something that she is doing and that we can see. Now let us consider an alternative statement: "Jane greets her customers with a smile and answers all their questions about the merchandise." Here we are dealing with an observable behavior: we can see her smiling and answering customers' questions. Keeping the focus on behavior accomplishes at least two objectives: making communications clearer and maintaining self-esteem. People are far more ready to listen to facts—observable events—than they are subjective interpretations.

SKILL PRACTICE EXERCISE 3
Identifying Behaviors

Some of the conditions in the list below are behaviors, and some are abstractions. Abstractions (personality traits, values, character qualities) do not tell us what the person has done to demonstrate the quality. Behaviors (laughing, walking, talking), on the other hand, are examples of performances and clearly indicate what the person is doing or has done. Place a check mark next to the behaviors.

___ **1.** Have a positive attitude.

___ **2.** Type a letter.

___ **3.** Interview an applicant for a job.

___ **4.** Be sincere.

___ **5.** Be a good employee.

___ **6.** Teach a job.

___ **7.** Work hard.

___ **8.** Feel proud of your company.

___ **9.** Enjoy your job.

___ **10.** Select the right tool.

___ **11.** Conduct a performance appraisal.

___ **12.** Perform confidently.

___ **13.** Place a check mark on this page.

___ **14.** Work conscientiously.

___ **15.** Investigate an accident.

___ **16.** Do your best.

___ **17.** Ask questions.

___ **18.** Show cooperation.

___ **19.** Maintain an open-minded point of view.

___ **20.** Read this page.

___ **21.** Concentrate on this exercise.

___ **22.** Come to work on time.

Answers

The following are behaviors: 2, 3, 6, 10, 11, 13, 15, 17, 20, 22.

SKILL PRACTICE EXERCISE 4
Focusing on Behavior

This exercise will help you develop skill in making statements that specifically focus on *behavior* rather than on attitudinal, personality, or other inappropriate dimensions. You will practice how a supervisor strengthens interactions with an employee by using specific, job-related statements rather than vague phrases so that the employee knows precisely what aspects of job performance are being referred to.

For each of the following attitudinal or personality statements write your own supervisory statement—one that *focuses on behavior* and that could be substituted on the job in a similar situation in your department.

1. *Supervisor:* Mary, I don't know what happened to your attitude. When you started to work here, you had a very good attitude. Now, all of a sudden, it's gone downhill. I want you to change your attitude.

_____

_____

_____

2. *Supervisor:* Betty, I don't know what in the world's the matter with you, but I'm going to have to have more initiative out of you. I know you can do better. Now, let's see more initiative out of you.

_____

_____

_____

3. *Supervisor:* Debbie, I really appreciate how efficient and self-starting you are. Thanks a lot.

_____

_____

_____

4. *Supervisor:* Bob, I just wanted to tell you that you're really doing a good job. You're really doing super. Just keep up the good work.

---

5. *Supervisor:* Edda, you really are ambitious. I want you to keep that up—with all the ambition you have, you're really going to go places.

---

6. *Supervisor:* Jack, I don't understand. Why are you so lazy?

---

7. *Supervisor:* Mitzi, why are you always disinterested in your work and in everything that goes on around here?

Answers

1. Mary, during the first month of your employment, you came to work on time each day. However, in the last 2 weeks you've been late three times.

2. Betty, whenever you finish an assignment, instead of waiting for me to tell you what to do next, please ask another employee in the department how you can be of assistance.

3. Debbie, I really appreciate how you are typically first to finish assignments and how you ask others if you can be of assistance.

4. Bob, I just wanted to tell you that you're doing a good job with the reports. You handed in all three on time, and each was complete. As a result, the accounting department was able to meet its deadline. Thanks—and I'm confident that you'll be able to continue this fine performance.

5. Edda, thanks for volunteering to come in and help out on Saturday. That's the kind of behavior that will help you build a career here.

6. Jack, why are you getting ready to clock out 10 minutes before the shift ends?

7. Mitzi, during the meeting you were the only one not taking notes. I was wondering why.

5

USING REINFORCEMENT TECHNIQUES TO SHAPE BEHAVIOR

One of the most crucial concepts in behavior modeling and, in turn, motivation is reinforcement. In virtually all the basic situations of life where human interactions occur—in supervisor-subordinate relationships, in child rearing, in marriages, in friendships, in classrooms—a knowledge of how to use reinforcement to shape behavior is necessary if a person wishes to have some control over how the situation will proceed. In the world of business, the ability to use reinforcement techniques is especially important. As we have seen, today's supervisors must be not only managers of time, budgets, and productivity but also managers of behavior.

BEHAVIOR AS A FUNCTION OF ITS CONSEQUENCES

For anyone who manages people, the bottom line is knowing how to encourage desirable behavior and discourage undesirable behavior. Simply defined, reinforcement is a key step in accomplishing this—a way of having someone associate a positive response with desirable acts and a negative response or no response with undesirable acts. The goal of this chapter is to elucidate some of the key techniques of behavior management and to give managers a solid sense of which ones are appropriate for which circumstances.

All behavior management techniques are based on the tested assumption that behavior is a function of its consequences. People are more likely to repeat an action if its consequences are pleasant, just as they are more likely not to repeat it if the consequences are unpleasant. The various consequences of an action reduce to four: positive reinforcement, negative reinforcement, punishment, and extinction. The first two of these tend to produce more of the given behavior, the last two less. All four represent strategies that a supervisor can use to change or strengthen employee performance. Let us consider each one briefly.

One way to increase the likelihood of a performance or behavior recurring is to follow that performance with a positive event. We call this technique positive reinforcement. A positively reinforced response has a greater probability of recurring simply because it pays off. Supervisory skills training places a heavy emphasis on positive reinforcement because of its proven utility: it is clear, direct, predictable, practical, and uncompromised by negative side effects.

The most obvious and simple example of positive reinforcement is the use of salary increases. A salesperson, for example, increases sales continually. The salesperson gets a raise and works even harder in order to elicit management's favorable response (in the form of a raise) again. A less tangible but nonetheless significant example of positive reinforcement can be seen with an employee who practices good housekeeping because the supervisor acknowledges it by telling the employee how important it is and how much it is appreciated. In all cases, positive reinforcement consists of the introduction of something rewarding *after* the behavior that is to be rewarded.

Another type of reward is the removal of something negative after the performance. In this case, the person is likely to repeat the behavior because something he or she doesn't like is taken away as a consequence of the behavior. We call this removal or elimination of adverse conditions negative reinforcement. The reinforcement comes from the withdrawal of a negative state.

To return to one of our previous examples, if an employee's good housekeeping effort stops a supervisor's angry complaints, then the behavior of good housekeeping is negatively reinforced. Notice that to negatively reinforce a performance is to promote it, not to discourage it. Although negative reinforcement is frequently confused with punishment, these are distinctly different techniques having opposite purposes. To ensure that we have clearly defined negative reinforcement, let us look at one more example. A division manager whose spending is constantly checked by senior management is able by year-end to stay within the budget. During the following budget period the division manager's budget is checked less often. Senior management has encouraged the desired action with a positive response by removing an unfavorable condition.

Now let us examine two strategies which produce less of a given behavior. The first and more obvious of these is punishment. Again, it is important to clarify that punishment is not the same as negative reinforcement. Whereas the latter actually encourages a performance, punishment means what it appears to mean, namely an attempt to decrease the chances of an undesirable performance recurring by following the performance with a distinctly unpleasant event. Thus a response is successfully punished when the punishment causes the behavior to decrease in frequency.

Examples of punishment are easy to conjure up: an employee is formally reprimanded for lateness; a middle manager is chastised for poor performance by a vice president at a board meeting; an administrative assistant is treated like a secretary because the supervisor is displeased with the assistant's work. Although punishment is heavily relied upon as a consequence of undesirable behavior, its utility is often dubious because of its negative side effects: more often than not, punishment makes an employee bitter, hostile, defensive, and prone to retaliation. Furthermore, the punished party often resumes the undesirable behavior as soon as the punishment stops. Punishment should therefore be used selectively instead of, as is usually the case, in a knee-jerk fashion.

The other basic technique for decreasing the likelihood of a behavior is extinction. With extinction, the undesirable performance is neither punished nor rewarded; it is simply ignored. There is no response to the behavior by the supervisor at all. Ignored behaviors tend to diminish (if the behaviors are not being rewarded by another source), and a behavior is ultimately extinguished as a result of a consistent lack of reinforcement.

To give an example of extinction, let us consider the supervisor who never acknowledges an employee's memos. Eventually, the employee will stop sending the memos because they are always ignored. If the supervisor did not want to keep receiving those memos (for whatever reason), the use of extinction as a technique for influencing behavior was effective. Often, however, this is not the case: many perfectly desirable performances are unintentionally extinguished by managers through carelessness. A manager should be aware of the potentially negative consequences of ignoring desired behavior. It should be added here that even when extinction is used consciously and appropriately, it is an imprecise technique: often positive behaviors (in addition to the negative ones) are ignored and are accidentally discouraged. Alternatives to extinction will be discussed further in this chapter.

POSITIVE REINFORCEMENT VERSUS PUNISHMENT

Before considering the conditions and intricacies of reinforcement, it is necessary to formulate an overall strategy. As a first step, let us confront the fundamental issue of positive reinforcement versus punishment. Despite the possibility of each strategy we have just defined leading in certain instances to a successful change or modification in employee performance, it is our position in this book that positive reinforcement is by far the most consistently successful and should be used most often. We say this with the full realization that punishment is the most popular method—that most managers consider it the most firm, practical, and called-for way to direct employees.

Actually, punishment is an unreliable method, especially when it is used to the exclusion of other alternatives. For the most part, the effects of punishment are unpredictable, whereas those of positive reinforcement are highly predictable. Put another way, punishment does not weaken behavior as much as positive reinforcement strengthens it. Although many supervisors will point to the alleged effectiveness of punishment, research shows that punishment has numerous negative side effects.

Let us consider some of these. First of all, punishment provides only a temporary decrease in undesirable behavior. While punishment initially stings the employee into cutting down the objectionable behavior, once the punishment consequence is withdrawn, the employee often resumes the undesirable behavior. Supervisors who stalk around reprimanding and punishing people must therefore be willing to assume the responsibilities of full-time police officers; they must continually be on the job in order to prevent the behavior from recurring if their choice of strategy is punishment.

A second disadvantage of punishment is that it increases the incidence of counterproductive emotional reactions. Often the behavior that is stopped by punishment is replaced by negative emotional reactions such as anger, hostility, aggression, frustration, fear, and withdrawal. As the supervisor, you may feel that the employee is getting what is deserved, and you may even take satisfaction in the employee's fear and defensiveness. But in the long run, as we have seen in previous chapters, these reactions do not motivate an employee to do a better job. On the contrary, they are profoundly unmotivating. Ultimately, a habitual use of punishment inhibits rather than enhances performance.

There are also more subtle side effects of punishment. Continually punishing an employee may, for example, permanently suppress the wrong response even when, in another context, it might be the right one. In other words, punishment can lead to blind and inflexible behavior. What is undesirable at one time may become highly desirable later on. But the employee who is punished and made to feel terrible in the first instance may not be able to make the transition; the employee may permanently adopt the desired behavior and use it even when inappropriate.

Another subtle and insidious side effect of the constant reliance on punishment is the way it can condition an employee to the employer. The supervisor who continually punishes people gets locked into a role. That supervisor becomes an authoritarian symbol—a cop with a billy club, a sour schoolteacher—who is seldom perceived by the employees in a positive context. Although the presence of what behavioral scientists call the "adverse stimulus" (in this case, the punishing supervisor) may motivate outward performance, in the long run the supervisor who becomes typed into a role of the "punisher" becomes ineffective because he or she is unable to positively reinforce. In addition, this seemingly "tough" role is actually weak and superficial in its overall impact: once the supervisor leaves the work setting, the control often vanishes.

This is not to say that punishment should never be used. On the contrary, there are instances where performance deficiencies or work habit problems merit punishment. What we *are* saying is that punishment should be used selectively, after other alternatives have been weighed. We are also saying that the effect of punishment is highly limited, especially in comparison with the effects of other techniques.

HOW CONSEQUENCES AFFECT BEHAVIOR

To illustrate the relative limitations and advantages of basic reinforcement techniques, let us take a sample employee through a series of scenarios which play various behaviors against possible consequences and probable outcomes. In the first instance, let us assume that we are dealing with an employee who shows off to coworkers, relays gossip and rumors, and tells obnoxious jokes. One way to deal with this behavior is simply to ignore it—consistently and resolutely. In this case, the response could be no response; the employee is attempting to get a rise out of us, and we make sure that the employee doesn't get it. This is an example of how ignoring a behavior can lead to its extinction if it is not being reinforced elsewhere. Behavior which is not reinforced at all tends to drop out or be pushed aside by behavior which is reinforced. If someone rattles on endlessly and meaninglessly, you might consider reacting with silence. In certain situations, no reaction at all can have a greater impact on reducing a behavior than any other type of reaction.

Now let us look at a more positive scenario. In this case, the employee seeks to gain recognition not through gossiping and showing off but through being cooperative with coworkers and demonstrating above-standard performance. An appropriate mode of response to this behavior is positive reinforcement: tell the employee that the job is being done well; explain why the work is good; express personal appreciation for the performance; and, if appropriate, give the employee a written commendation. The probable outcome is that the reinforcement will lead to a repetition of the above-standard performance. What is particularly gratifying about positive reinforcement is this: If we selectively reward desirable employee behavior, that behavior will not only occur with more frequency in the future but will become a habitual method for satisfying the employee's needs. It thus becomes a mutually satisfying and therefore long-sustaining mechanism. Unlike other methods, positive reinforcement has staying power.

Now let us consider the less pleasant scenario of the employee who grumbles to coworkers, initiates petty rumors, and is performing below standard. In this case, a reprimand from the supervisor may indeed be appropriate. Chances are the employee will suspend the dysfunctional behavior—but only when the supervisor is around. The supervisor should be aware of this limitation and, in addition to the reprimand, look for a way to begin positively reinforcing the employee's desirable behavior—if any—so that a more comprehensive change can occur. The thing to remember about punishment is this: Behavior which leads to a reprimand will be temporarily avoided, at least under the same situation, but desirable behavior will not by itself occur. What will occur if punishment is used excessively is a dynamic of retaliation by the punished employee: grievances, stealing, and absenteeism are frequent by-products of punishment.

Finally, let us look at the worker who tries to gain recognition by working more efficiently. We might say to the worker, "Now you don't have to take work home." This is an example of negative reinforcement which leads to a repetition of the positive performance. Behavior which is followed by the removal of an annoying event will most likely be repeated.

SCULPTING BEHAVIOR

Having looked at several scenarios of how various modes of reinforcement operate in concrete situations, let us now consider some of the basic conditions for successful schedules of reinforcement. Some of these are subtle; others are simple common sense. But all of them are necessary if the manager wishes to be a systematic and successful sculptor of behavior. We are using this metaphor intentionally: a manager is precisely a sculptor in that he or she must shape the basic materials—in this case the behavior of employees—to achieve the desired product.

A problem with the shaping principles we shall now discuss is that for many of us they do not come naturally. Rather, they must be applied consciously, carefully, and systematically. Most managers are far better at punishing. In our schools, our homes, and our businesses we are provided with models who rely on criticism. We are not as a matter of course taught to deal with performance problems any other way. Some managers make up for this lack of reinforcement expertise by instinctively playing the skills they do have for everything they're worth: they set high goals, or utilize effective training skills, or have unusual experience—or simply work hard. In other words, they learn how to survive in spite of their inability to efficiently generate performance change. On the other hand, it is often the case that they do not survive at all.

In any case, a mastery of the basic principles of shaping behavior is invaluable to any manager who wishes to successfully influence behavior—but it must be a thoughtful and systematic process.

To begin with, the manager should recognize that it is more difficult to initiate change than to sustain it; therefore, a supervisor should apply more reinforcement at the outset—when employees are furthest from the goal. This is the fundamental strategy for beginning any shaping process.

Managers frequently make the basic mistake of looking for an excessively large unit of behavior to begin the process of reinforcement. It is more sensible to begin with small pieces and build from there. Furthermore, when initiating a behavior change, it is necessary to remember that you must reinforce *very frequently* at the beginning. If you allow the initial responses to go unrewarded, even the small ones, they will often not be sustained.

It should be noted that this principle applies to other behavior consequences. The manager should react to the first sign of desirable or undesirable behavior rather than wait for behavior to be repeated and become pronounced. If a worker begins to do something well, the manager should reward that behavior quickly or it may vanish; if the worker does something negative, the manager should deal with it quickly or it may recur and become a serious problem. A second principle to remember is that the manager's response, whether in reinforcing or in punishing, must come *after* the behavior rather than before it. If the reinforcement comes before, it will not necessarily shape the behavior. This principle has a wide application. If a father and mother, for example, want their teenager to mow the lawn, they increase the chances of getting the lawn mowed by telling their child that the car can be borrowed after the job is done, not before.

A corollary to this principle is that the closer the consequence is to the behavior, the greater is the impact. Reinforcement should follow *immediately* after the desired response. Salary raises are a case in point: *annual* increases may prevent an employee from leaving the company, but they often do not move the employee to produce more because they are too removed from the immediate act. Far more reinforcing is a raise which follows immediately after a specific performance. The connection must be made clear.

What we are saying in behavioral terms is that reinforcement must be "response-contingent." The performance and the reward should be clearly associated with each other. Otherwise, the impact of the reinforcement is blunted, or the response is simply confusing. Here are a few additional pointers: Reinforce every early response and every improvement, however slight. Later, let reinforcement come intermittently—but do this gradually. As behavior increases in frequency and as long as it is at desired levels, the supervisor can gradually, not abruptly, reduce the schedule. Only after the basic behavior and its pattern of reward have been established should the reinforcement taper off. When the pattern is in place, the manager can then periodically and randomly reward the behavior. Indeed, after the behavior increases to the desired level, the manager should be unpredictable in the frequency of reinforcement.

The rationale for random scheduling after the objective has been reached needs clarification. At this point, the reader might well ask, "If the more you reinforce, the higher will be the rate of behavior, then why make the response random? Won't the behavior then become random?" The answer is that randomness of response should be instituted only after the positive behavior pattern is firmly established. To look at it another way, if the reward is offered every Monday, the performance will soon be better on Monday but not during the rest of the week. Paradoxically, once the behavior has been acquired, the random response-contingent reinforcement becomes the very one which generates the greater predictability and consistency.

While the behavior is in the acquisition stage, however, the manager should not worry about overdoing the reinforcement. In business and industry, the problem of people getting tired of being reinforced too much is theoretical and virtually irrelevant. The characteristic problem is too little reinforcement, not too much.

If you think you have been following these principles and an employee's performance nevertheless deteriorates, the crucial questions to ask yourself are "When was the behavior last reinforced?" and "What was the general frequency of reinforcement recently?" You will find in a high percentage of the cases either a sharp reduction in reinforcement or an actual cessation. It should also be noted that the employee's performance deficiency may be a result of third-party reinforcement—from a shop steward or from coworkers, for example.

Unfortunately, there are no neatly codified rules to memorize in determining the precise schedule of reinforcement for a given situation. Schedules are situational: they should be determined by measuring the actual response, not by any predetermined rule. What works helps to determine what should be continued.

There is another condition of reinforcement that must be considered: the manager must make sure that positive and negative responses are seen as such by the recipient. No one reward or punishment is suitable for everyone. The person who is on the receiving end is the determiner of whether a given consequence is rewarding or punishing.

Management's frequent failure to sort out what is really rewarding for whom has been at the root of many productivity problems. Ironically, the best employees are often the most punished because their supervisors often "reward" them with monotonous or unpleasant jobs that poorer-performing employees might protest. In a further twist of irony, the mediocre workers get rewarded because they don't get the undesirable jobs. The upshot is that the manager is left with third-rate people after the first-rate ones have had the sense to bail out.

The whole issue of misperceived or distorted rewards and punishments is complex and fascinating. In their book *Analyzing Performance Problems*, Robert F. Mager and Peter Pipe (1970) identify four reasons why people frequently don't do what they ought to do:

1. It's punishing to do it.

2. It's rewarding not to do it.

3. The performance doesn't really matter one way or the other.

4. There are obstacles to performing.

The first of these, punishment for superior performance, we have already mentioned. Examples of this perverse phenomenon are frequent. Perhaps the most stereotypical one is the "A" student who, having often been jeered and identified as the teacher's pet or the intellectual by anti-intellectual classmates, begins to make mediocre grades. In this case, the "reward" for excellence is so unpleasant that the individuals opt for mediocrity. Another example concerns the secretaries who are rewarded for doing too much work for too many different people—a case of overload which they of course loathe—and have even more work dumped on them by more people because of the good job they do. If they quit, their various bosses shouldn't really wonder why. When confronted with a situation in which an employee seems to know how to perform but doesn't, a manager should try to determine whether the desired performance actually has negative consequences—not for the manager, but for the *employee*. Is it in the *employee's* interest to do the job that isn't getting done? If not, the manager might consider alternatives. Are there ways to do away with the negative consequences and create positive ones?

A similar debacle is the situation in which doing nothing is the most rewarding thing to do. The workplace is full of cases where the individuals in charge don't tell people under them how to properly do their jobs because they remain the only ones who know what is going on and thus retain power and status. An especially ludicrous example of rewards not being linked to the desired performance concerns the publish or perish ethic in university teaching: professors get promoted or receive tenure not because of their effectiveness as teachers but because of their publications and committee work. They are expected to be good teachers, but they get no reward for it. Indeed, they are better off *not* putting their energies into teaching, since those very energies can be channeled more expediently into getting published. The principle here is that managers must continually ask themselves what a worker gets out of a desired performance. If, after putting themselves in the employee's shoes, managers perceive that the desired performance really confers no rewards, they need to create some without delay.

A closely related scenario is one in which *nothing* happens as a consequence of a desired performance. An employee who realizes that it doesn't matter whether a job is done right or wrong may well do it wrong. People who persist in being late, for example, may do so because there is neither a reprimand for it nor an award for being punctual. Managers should be careful to attach consequences to desired actions, to make the performance matter.

A final area for a manager to consider in this regard is obstacles. If an employee who knows the correct performance is not measuring up, the problem may be that there is no reward system in place because there are too many obstacles to making the performance achievable. A good case in point is again provided by the harassed secretaries who work for more than one boss and who must meet the often conflicting demands of them all. They may *want* to do a good job, but they are effectively prevented from doing it by the very people they are working for. A removal of these obstructions would be an excellent "reward."

It cannot be emphasized too strongly that errors in the shaping of behavior have concrete, sometimes devastating consequences. We are not discussing a superficial embellishment but a basic component of good business. Reinforcement matters. Take as an example the young employee who comes in late and explains that the car had to be dug out of the snow. The employee smiles eagerly, anticipating commendation. The supervisor frowns in frustration at the lateness. The supervisor has followed desirable behavior with a negative response. Next snowstorm, the employee is more likely to stay home. Even no response would have been wrong in that situation. Indeed, failure to commend good performance is management's most common mistake in motivation. Almost without exception, good performance that is unnoticed deteriorates.

We should also make clear that reinforcement has upward as well as downward utility and should by no means be thought of solely in terms of management dealings with employees. It can work the other way too. Suppose, for example, a pedantic committee chairperson drones on endlessly, wasting valuable time. The committee members are annoyed, but, following tradition, each congratulates the chairperson when the meeting ends. The committee has followed an undesirable act with a positive response, encouraging the chairperson to drone on next time.

SUMMARY OF KEY REINFORCEMENT CONCEPTS

Since reinforcement is so crucial in so many contexts, let us summarize once again the key concepts.

1. The primary result of using reinforcement is that performance improves because there is an increase in the frequency of the desired behavior.

2. The major effect of not using reinforcement is that performance either does not improve or gets worse.

3. The side effects of criticism or punishment are:

   a. Defensive behavior

   b. Hostility, anger, a loss of motivation

   c. Sabotaging or retaliatory acts

4. As you begin positive reinforcement, you must recognize what is done well even in limited performance areas and reward it.

5. You must reward each improvement in performance until the desired level is achieved; then reinforce from time to time.

6. If existing good performance and each step of improved performance are not rewarded, the desired behavior will probably not be achieved.

7. To establish or strengthen desired behavior, you must increase the amount of positive reinforcement.

8. To eliminate undesired behavior, you must stop reinforcement.

9. In general, a behavior should be reinforced at least twice a week until it is established.

The importance of these concepts for the business world has been so frequently documented that managers are simply not in a position to ignore them. One company estimates that 50 percent of its performance problems are due to the absence of or inadequate use of reinforcement.

SKILL PRACTICE EXERCISE 5
Reinforcement Techniques

The scenes in this exercise illustrate various reinforcement techniques. To Improve your understanding of these techniques, read each scene carefully and then answer the questions related to it.

Scene 1

Supervisor: Jack, I want you to know that I appreciate the job you do on the seam busting. When the garments get to the hemmers, they have no problem with the seams because they're always open.

Employee: Thanks, Barbara. It's nice to know when you're doing a good job.

1. What type of reinforcement is the employee's supervisor using?

_____

_____

_____

2. How did the supervisor make the employee feel?

_____

_____

3. What is the employee likely to do in the future?

_____

_____

4. Is the supervisor likely to compliment the employee in the future? Why?

_____

_____

_____

Scene 2

Employee: Jim, since you told us to be on the lookout for the bolt threads, we've been picking up 10 percent more defects during the last two shifts.

Supervisor: Yeah, but I'm looking for Joe. Did you see him?

1. What type of behavior consequence is this supervisor displaying?

_____

2. What do you predict will be the result of the supervisor's response?

_____

_____

3. If you were the supervisor in this situation, what would you say?

_____

_____

Scene 3

Employee: Jim, since you told us to be on the lookout, we've been picking up 10 percent more bolt defects during the last two shifts.

Supervisor: Great! You guys are really getting quality-conscious. I'm glad to hear it. I know I can rely on you to do the best possible job.

1. What effect is the supervisor's comment likely to have on the employee's future motivation?

_____

_____

2. Which method increases the chances of maintaining the number of defects picked up?

_____

Scene 4

Employee: Hey, Tom, I just finished getting this shaft out of the bearing. Now we can begin to finish repairing the pump.

Supervisor: You mean to tell me it took you 2 damn hours just to press that thing out of there?

1. How did the supervisor make the employee feel?

_____

2. What is the employee likely to do in the future?

_____

_____

3. If you were the supervisor, what would you have said?

_____

_____

Scene 5

Employee: I'm damn bored. All I do every day is just break down these damn pumps.

Supervisor: Well, Steve, you know that once you learn all the fundamentals of these small pieces of equipment, you'll be able to advance to the larger pieces. You *are* going to learn more. Each day you'll pick up something that you didn't know before, and pretty soon you'll be working with the larger equipment.

1. What reinforcement principle is being demonstrated?

_____

2. How did the employee feel before speaking to the supervisor?

_____

3. How did the employee feel after speaking to the supervisor?

_____

Scene 6

Supervisor: Sandy, I gave you a verbal warning 2 weeks ago concerning your absence problem, but I see that you've missed 3 more days. Now the only alternative I have is to give you a written reprimand.

1. What type of consequence is the supervisor using?

_____

2. What is the employee likely to do in the future?

_____

Scene 7

Supervisor: Sandy, if during the next 60 days you can achieve and maintain a perfect attendance record, I'll be happy to remove this written reprimand from your personnel file.

Employee: Oh, I didn't know that you're able to do that.

1. What type of reinforcement is the supervisor using?

_____

_____

2. What is the employee likely to do in the future?

_____

Scene 8

Employee 1: I hear you got your report out last night, despite everything you had to do. I'll bet Fred was happy.

Employee 2: Oh, he didn't say anything about it. It was as if he didn't even care. But that's the way he is. He never says anything.

1. What behavioral consequence did Fred, the supervisor, use?

_____

2. What are the employees likely to do in the future?

_____

3. If you were the supervisor in this situation, how would you have handled it?

_____

_____

_____

Scene 9

Supervisor: Joe, you did a great job cleaning the chips from the machines the last two Friday nights. I appreciate it, and I want you to do it every Friday night from now on.

Employee: (*Anger.*)

1. What happened to the employee for doing his job well?

_____

2. Do you think he'll be more or less motivated to clean the equipment in the future?

_____

Answers

Scene 1

1. Positive reinforcement—a reward that increases the likelihood that the behavior will be repeated.

2. Proud, confident, happy, competent.

3. Continue to do more of the behavior that was praised.

4. Yes. The employee positively reinforced the supervisor.

Scene 2

1. Extinction–ignoring the employee.

2. Decreased employee effectiveness; less motivation.

3. Congratulations, Tom. I knew I could count on you. Keep up the good work.

Scene 3

1. Motivation will be increased, or at least maintained.

2. Second–positive reinforcement.

Scene 4

1. Punished, incompetent, like a child, guilty.

2. Less effective work, less communication, less competent work.

3. Good, John. I know it's a messy job, and I'm glad you completed it. The average time for completing the job is 1 hour, so let's talk about how you can accomplish that as well.

Scene 5

1. Negative–removal of an adverse condition.

2. Bored, unmotivated, unproductive; minimal self-esteem.

3. Optimistic, involved, motivated, purposeful.

Scene 6

1. Punishment. Introducing an adverse condition to decrease the undesirable behavior—absence.

2. Decrease her absences. But unless the employee's feelings are also dealt with (see Chapter 6), negative side effects may develop.

Scene 7

1. Negative reinforcement—removal of an adverse condition to increase attendance.

2. Increase her attendance.

Scene 8

1. Ignoring the behavior.

2. Be less motivated and less productive.

3. Recognized and praised the employee's achievement to maximize self-confidence and a feeling of competence and to make the employee aware of my appreciation for productivity.

Scene 9

1. First he was praised, and then he received punishment.

2. Less motivated.

6

USING ACTIVE LISTENING
TO SHOW UNDERSTANDING

As we have seen, one of management's greatest challenges is the need to influence and change the behavior of others. The effective manager—the one who generates high productivity in a conscious and consistent manner—is the one who knows how to manage the behavior of subordinates without subverting the relationship or damaging self-esteem. In other words, the successful manager is the one whose vision is not self-centered, who sees that the production needs of the company are precisely consistent with the human needs of the personnel.

An invaluable tool that can aid the supervisor in effectively communicating with subordinates is the skill of active listening. This is a skill which has several simultaneous functions: it reduces defensiveness, promotes self-esteem, and defuses emotional exchanges. It also aids in ensuring clarity—the foundation of all good communication—and in general enhances the relationship between the supervisor and the employee. The purpose of this chapter is to define active listening and give the reader a real life sense of how it functions through exercises taken from common work situations.

A DEFINITION

Briefly defined, active listening is the ability to pick up, define, and respond accurately to the feelings expressed by the other person; it is learning to really listen, without butting in or projecting one's own opinion and ego. If an employee is angry and frustrated, the supervisor who actively listens may well defuse that anger and turn it around toward motivated behavior.

BENEFITS OF ACTIVE LISTENING

Before going further to examine the specific dynamics of active listening, let us look at a few typical on-the-job situations. In previous chapters, we have seen that basic behavior principles are often ignored in management. This is because the principles of motivation usually go against the grain of our upbringing; we behave on the job the way we were taught to behave by our parents, often to the point of treating our employees like children. Nowhere is the destructive and demeaning dynamic more apparent than in the inability of managers to listen.

Take the hypothetical case of a frustrated jobber who comes in to see a manufacturer. Gesturing in near desperation, the jobber says, "I can't take it anymore! This is the third price increase in 2 years. They'll promote items from the other divisions. My division will never match last year's sales. What the hell are we supposed to do?" The typical manager in this situation probably would not have let the jobber get this far; the manager probably would have interrupted the jobber with a hostile interjection. Even if the jobber is allowed to finish complaining, the manager will probably shrug or come back with a counterblast without acknowledging what the jobber has said.

The typical reaction of a manager in this situation is to assume the role of an outraged parent. The manager doesn't listen; the manager just reacts—either coldly and abruptly or at length, in a long-winded sermon. If the jobber in our example is met with either reaction, the response will be increased anger and defensiveness. Even worse, the jobber will feel that the manager is not listening. There is little chance that this interaction will lead to a productive conversation. Furthermore, the jobber will probably retaliate against the manufacturer later on in a meeting with coworkers. The consequence of not listening is a chain reaction of alienation and hostility which can only sabotage sales.

But suppose the manufacturer chooses to respond this way to the jobber's complaint: "You think our pricing isn't realistic, so your salespeople won't even try to sell our line, and you're

discouraged because this might hurt your division's sales."
Such a response goes a long way toward lessening the other
party's anger and frustration and creates a context for further
discussion. The jobber executive will be satisfied that the manufacturer is actually listening and understanding. Most important, the jobber will then be more open to the manufacturer's
explanation about the price increase.

The principle practiced in the second scenario is active listening. The manager feeds back the emotionally charged information that the jobber has given and the feelings expressed.
When this principle is employed, the person with the problem
perceives that he or she is being understood. This perception
frees the person to explore his or her own feelings, to express
personal ideas, and to rely less on defensive behavior.

Active listening is a communication technique that is utilized in virtually every behavior model in the section to follow.
The effects of active listening are as follows:

1. *There is a comforting effect for the person being actively listened to.* In some of the models presented in
   the final section of this book, you will see an employee
   expressing volatile emotions. Many times just verbal-
   izing these feelings of bitterness or frustration clears
   the air and allows the employee to resume working
   almost as if nothing had happened. If this sounds silly
   or mystical, try it the next time you hear a vociferous
   complaint. Try it especially if you are not in the habit
   of doing it. You may be surprised.

2. *Active listening promotes rapport between supervisor
   and employee.* You will notice later on in this book
   that the experience of being heard and understood is
   so satisfying that rapport can be achieved and is more
   easily achieved. As we have already seen, a positive
   relationship—or at least a friendly, mutually respectful
   connection—between supervisor and employee is not
   just a pleasant frill but is good for business. But there

is another reason why active listening makes good business sense. In general, active listening encourages employees to think for themselves, to diagnose their own problems, and to discover their own solutions. Employees who feel that they are being understood and respected as competent people will feel better about themselves and will put more confidence in their own judgments. Correspondingly, they will feel that the manager trusts them to think for themselves. Active listening conveys this trust and is one of the most effective ways of helping a subordinate become self-directing, responsible, and independent. An employee who feels that he or she has an ownership in solutions to problems will value those solutions more than an employee who feels treated like a child or a pawn.

HOW TO ACTIVELY LISTEN

Now let us summarize the steps in active listening. We are not talking about some mystical mode of empathy but about a communication skill that can be learned and practiced. Through day-to-day practice, a skillful and consistent use of this technique can be developed. The process is rather simple: in active listening, the supervisor attempts to understand what the employee is feeling or what the employee's message means. Then the supervisor transposes the message into his or her own words and feeds it back to the employee for verification. It is important to emphasize that the supervisor utilizing this skill does not send a message of his or her own—no interjections, opinion, advice, or sermon. The supervisor should feed back only what the subordinate's message means, in both content and emotion.

Active listening is thus a specific, nondirective behavioral skill. It is used in a variety of contexts. In parent-effectiveness training, for example, the parent is told to simply listen at the outset and to make judgments for the child later. In hot-line training, the trainee is told that if a suicide calls, the first thing to do is be empathetic.

Let's look at another example, this time for a work situation. An angry plant manager slaps the conference table and says,

"You give me impossible schedules, and you refuse to pay overtime. I'm supposed to be a magician." The vice president for manufacturing could fire back a blistering retort—or simply choose to nod and say, "You think we're asking too much. You're angry because we don't seem to recognize your problems or care about them." The vice president who chooses the latter course is practicing active listening and makes the plant manager feel understood by saying something calming but not condescending and thus creates possibilities for further discussion. If the former course is chosen, the vice president is promoting alienation and confrontation—not exactly the optimum conditions for a productive discussion.

Active listening is therefore a process which consists of three component parts:

1. *Acceptance:* The supervisor listens without interrupting and passes no value judgments.

2. *Clarification:* The supervisor captures the employee's feeling and understands why the employee is feeling that way.

3. *Feedback:* The supervisor feeds back how he or she thinks the employee is feeling and why.

It should be emphasized that active listening is conceptually simple but sometimes difficult in practice. The fulfillment of all parts of the process, especially in emotionally heightened situations, can take considerable discipline on the listener's part. Indeed, listening is an *active* process, not a passive one— thus the term "active listening."

We should clarify at this point that we do not have only angry or frustrated employees in mind when we advocate active listening. This is a skill which is equally valuable in pleasant situations. If an employee has good news to report, say "That's terrific!" and feed back the information in an animated and enthusiastic way. This response will reinforce the employee's positive feelings and encourage a repetition of the situation which produced them. We have emphasized negative situations because they cause the most difficulty and have the potential for considerable damage. But active listening can be used in positive as well as negative situations. It is certainly as important to promote good feelings as it is to defuse bad ones.

When feelings are vague and are barely being conveyed, active listening can be a most appropriate and powerful means of stimulating the employee to express the feelings fully. Keep in mind that for the employee "feelings are facts" and that unless they are dealt with or at the very least recognized, solving emotional problems is not likely to take place.

We should also emphasize that active listening can be used for upward communication as well. The boss is as likely to fly off the handle as anyone else, and it doesn't hurt to have some notion of how to calm the boss down. In fact, all the general principles that have been discussed can be used in upward and lateral communication as well as in downward communication.

WORDS THAT DESCRIBE FEELINGS

Depression

Lonely
Depressed
Lost
Empty
Discouraged
Rejected
Helpless
Disappointed
Hurt
Crushed
Drained
Vulnerable
Used
Confused
Bored
Shy

Abused
Down
Sad

Anger, Hostility

Mad
Angry
Hostile
Furious
Hate
Bitter
Irritated
Resentful
Jealous
Envious
Disgusted
Cheated

Agitated
Upset
Offended
Slighted

Happiness, Joy

Happy
Amused
Delighted
Pleased
Cheerful
Grateful
Surprised
Relieved
Hopeful
Enthusiastic
Elated

Glad
Excited
Turned on

Fear, Anxiety

Panicky
Frightened
Anxious
Threatened
Scared
Worried
Afraid
Nervous

**Inadequacy
(Negative self-esteem)**

Embarrassed
Ashamed
Humiliated
Guilty

Insecure
Ignored
Neglected
Doubtful
Unimportant
Regretful
Unsure
Intimidated
Uncertain
Left out
Unappreciated

**Adequacy
(Positive self-esteem)**

Competent
Confident
Determined
Proud
Fulfilled
Capable
Needed

Secure
Important
Appreciated

Care, Loving

Caring
Loving
Sympathy
Pity

Frustration

Blocked
Trapped
Burdened
Smothered
Overwhelmed
Frustrated
Torn
Driven
Exasperated

SKILL PRACTICE EXERCISE 6
Active Listening

Below are some statements made by employees. Read each statement carefully and then select the response that best represents *active listening*. Keep in mind that an *active listening* response offers no advice or opinion. It simply captures how the employee is *feeling* and *why*. Place a check mark next to the response that best represents *active listening*.

Employee	Supervisor's active listening response
1. They always get the easy jobs, and you save the hard ones for me.	____ **a.** What evidence do you have for that?
	____ **b.** You're forgetting about yesterday when I gave you the easy job.
	____ **c.** You feel that I'm picking on you and that I'm unfair about the way I assign work.
	____ **d.** If you would carefully analyze the work schedule, you would see that hard and easy jobs are equally assigned.
2. This is the type of work I can really sink my teeth into. I get so wrapped up in it that I can forget when to go home. The salary is OK and the working conditions are fine, but it's the work itself that motivates me the most.	____ **a.** That's the kind of attitude we like to see around here.
	____ **b.** I can understand that because that's how I feel about my job.
	____ **c.** Would you like to do more of this type of work?
	____ **d.** The work you're doing really stimulates and excites you.

3. When I first joined this company, I really thought I was going to get somewhere. Well, I've been working here 5 years, and I'm still in the same job.

_____ a. Getting ahead is important to you. You're disappointed in your progress.

_____ b. Be patient, and soon it will be your turn to advance.

_____ c. Let's talk about the things you can do to place yourself in a better position to be promoted.

_____ d. Maybe it's because you haven't worked hard enough.

4. Around here everybody is your boss. First I try to satisfy Mr. Jones's requests, and then Mr. Green asks me to do something, and sometimes even Mr. Smith gives me assignments. I just can't keep all of them happy. Most of the time I don't know what I should be doing.

_____ a. Take things a step at a time, and before you know it, everything will be done.

_____ b. Now try not to get so upset. After all, you're doing an excellent job.

_____ c. With all these people giving you things to do at one time, you must feel like you're being pulled in all directions. It's really getting you down.

_____ d. I didn't know Mr. Smith was giving you assignments. Let me find out what's going on, and then I'll get back to you.

5. There I was relying on you at the meeting. I thought you would be supporting my position. Instead, all you did was sit there. You didn't open your mouth once!

_____ a. There were some pretty good reasons for my keeping quiet at the meeting.

_____ b. You're kind of disgusted with the way I handled myself at the meeting.

_____ c. Joe, I contributed information two or three times at that meeting. I guess you just didn't hear me.

_____ **d.** I was waiting for you to call on me.

6. Hey, the bulletin board has a letter from the president congratulating our department on meeting all our objectives.

_____ **a.** It feels pretty good to get some recognition from the top.

_____ **b.** Yeah, I know. But don't let it go to your head.

_____ **c.** Really? I'd better go read it.

_____ **d.** Exactly what did the letter say?

7. It's the same thing day in and day out. So far as I'm concerned, a 10-year-old can do this.

_____ **a.** You're not going to get anywhere by complaining.

_____ **b.** If you have any ideas on how to make the job more interesting, why don't you submit them.

_____ **c.** I always thought you liked your job.

_____ **d.** The repetitive work is boring and makes you feel underutilized and unimportant.

8. Solve one problem and up pops another. What's the use?

_____ **a.** Look, it's just part of the job. No use getting upset about it.

_____ **b.** I'm surprised you feel that way.

_____ **c.** Give me some specific examples so I know exactly what you are talking about.

_____ **d.** It's frustrating and even discouraging to encounter problem after problem.

Answers

1. c, 2. d, 3. a, 4. c, 5. b, 6. a, 7. d, 8. d.

SKILL PRACTICE EXERCISE 7
Identifying the Feeling

Below are some typical statements made by employees on the job. Read each statement carefully—concentrate only on the feeling, not on the content and not on the situation in which the statement might occur. In the right-hand column write the feelings you think are being conveyed.

Employee's statement	Employee's feeling
example: All I ever do around here is clean up after part-timers.	Fed up, annoyed, angry
1. Nobody seems to care about what the workers have to say.	_____
2. I understand the new rule, but the old rules have so many exceptions.	_____
3. I don't believe it! You're assigning that job to me again?	_____
4. She's a good supervisor; she's fair.	_____
5. It seems like a good idea, but I just don't know.	_____
6. You know, I read the new employee manual, but it's so long, and I don't think it's written very clearly.	_____
7. My hands are tied—unless I get the equipment I need, I can't do the job.	_____
8. Five lousy minutes! You're carrying on because I was ready to leave 5 minutes early!	_____

Answers
1. Ignored, neglected, unimportant, discouraged
2. Confused, discouraged

3. Amazed, bothered, ticked off
4. Pleased, content, satisfied
5. Unsure, uncertain, doubtful
6. Overwhelmed, frustrated, exasperated
7. Stymied, frustrated, in a bind, mad
8. Surprised, caught, annoyed, mad

SKILL PRACTICE EXERCISE 8
Determining Message Feeling and Content

Now that you have identified the feelings being expressed, try to determine the content of each message. By putting feelings and content together, you are listening actively. In the right-hand column write a supervisor's response for each statement. Include both feeling and content (cause for the feeling) in each response.

Employee's statement	Your response
example: All I ever do around here is clean up after part-timers.	You're really fed up with doing work that you think belongs to them.
1. Nobody seems to care about what the workers have to say.	
2. I understand the new rule, but the old rules have so many exceptions.	
3. I don't believe it! You're assigning that job to me again?	
4. She's a good supervisor; she's fair.	
5. It seems like a good idea, but I just don't know.	
6. You know, I read the new employee manual, but it's so long, and I don't think it's written very clearly.	
7. My hands are tied—unless I get the equipment I need, I can't do the job.	
8. Five lousy minutes! You're carrying on because I was ready to leave 5 minutes early!	

Answers

1. It's discouraging and frustrating for you not to have a say in things.

2. You're confused by so many variations in the rules

3. My asking you to do that report over bothers you.

4. You're satisfied to be working for such a fair boss.

5. You're unsure about the whole idea.

6. You're overwhelmed by so much material, and the way it is written is confusing.

7. Not having the right equipment is frustrating and puts you in a bind.

8. My bringing this to your attention really ticks you off and makes you mad.

7

SETTING SOLID GOALS AND MAINTAINING COMMUNICATION

According to a recent study published by the American Management Association, one of the most frequent and damaging on-the-job sources of executive stress is "a lack of feedback on one's job performance." The report defines "feedback" in a comprehensive way: what people at work find stressful is a lack of *any* communication, whether positive or negative, praise or criticism. This phenomenon occurs at all levels of the work force. From vice presidents to secretaries, workers frequently perceive themselves as operating in a void, with no clear knowledge of whether they are performing well or poorly or what they are really supposed to be performing in the first place.

Our present chapter offers an antidote to this discouraging situation by providing supervisors with a method of setting concrete goals and following them up with periodic communication. Such a method is crucial if the principles of motivation we have previously discussed—building self-esteem, focusing on specific problems, reinforcing desired behavior, and actively listening—are to be implemented over a long span of time. The process works both ways: in a successful use of goal setting and feedback the application of our other four principles of motivation is taken as a given, and those principles must be continually placed within a larger context of goal setting and communication.

COMPONENTS OF GOAL SETTING

With this larger framework in mind, let us begin with goal setting. One of the most interesting and surprising findings of recent research is that the common injunction to "do your best" is virtually useless in motivating people. Actually, if we think about it, this finding is not surprising at all. We have already seen in Chapter 4 that vagueness is the archenemy of productivity. What does "do your best" mean? To the worker, faced with numerous variables, it can mean dozens of things—and since the worker hears it all the time, it comes to mean nothing at all.

Our position is simple: goals should be specific, clearly stated, and clearly measurable. Goals which fulfill these criteria provide a source of feedback, accountability, and evaluation. Well-stated, measurable objectives are invaluable in motivating people and improving their performance. It is common sense that if an employee does not have a clear idea of the task at hand and does not receive feedback on the performance of it, he or she cannot realistically be held accountable for it. Nevertheless, it is a sad fact that the chaotic office where no one really knows what to do and very few ever get feedback on what is or is not being done effectively is more the rule than the exception.

Let's be even more concrete. Sound objectives have three identifiable elements:

1. An action verb ("to increase," for example)

2. A measurable result (such as "five or more per day")

3. The date by which the objective will be accomplished

Do not say, "I want you to get your work done soon." Instead, say, "The goal is to increase production 10 percent by June 16th." And whatever you do, avoid saying, "Why don't we get together sometime soon and discuss this again." Rather, say, "Let's get together on March 3d at 3 o'clock for a review of our progress."

This last point is crucial. Some managers set goals but fail to follow through with the necessary monitoring for their attainment. It is important to be clear not only about the content of a goal and the target date for its completion but about dates for discussion as work progresses. This principle applies in any situation. A good teacher, for example, doesn't say, "I want you to show me your term paper sometime soon." A good teacher says, "Bring in the introduction in 3 weeks—on Friday, April 15th." The point is to keep in touch and keep reviewing the project or problem. This point brings us back to some of our earlier techniques. By specifying a time to review the matter at hand, the supervisor can provide a practical structure for interacting with the employee as well as an ideal opportunity for reevaluation, reinforcement, and continued communication.

In the process of maintaining communication, it is essential to keep in mind the principles of motivation discussed earlier. Specifically, be sure to actively listen to the employee and to enhance the employee's self-esteem at every appropriate point. Since people tend to live up to their self-perceptions, your most important contribution will be building the other person's confidence so that the person can achieve the goal. Reinforcement is of course a vital part of this process; when the employee demonstrates a desired behavior, especially in the beginning, he or she should be immediately reinforced to encourage a repetition and a strengthening of that behavior.

Being "the boss," the supervisor is in the ideal position to make this process work. The supervisor can speak up and make use of his or her high-potency position to encourage the kind of open communications that are so frequently necessary for effective solutions to on-the-job problems. As we have noted earlier, the supervisor's efforts should be directed toward helping the employee to talk more freely and to offer personal reactions, opinions, suggestions, and ideas in a nondefensive manner. The entire interaction should be geared toward building self-esteem, self-confidence, competency, and personal involvement.

Indeed, we are convinced that supervisors are most successful in motivating employees when they learn to elicit employee feelings, thoughts, and ideas *before* offering their own. Research consistently shows that self-motivated, self-directed performance is performance which can be counted on. Consequently, managers should talk less and listen more, even when an employee is upset. Rather than saying to an employee,

"You're upset; take a while to calm down and then come back and we'll talk," the manager should actively listen, focus on the problem, and help the employee arrive at a solution. The flow of information from workers should be maximized: managers should encourage employee to talk more, first, and then talk less, second, themselves. For managers, this may be a tall order, but it is a style of behavior which is well worth learning and practicing at the workplace, especially when things are not getting done.

In addition to clarity and follow-through, the question of standards comes into play when considering how to set goals. How difficult or demanding should goals be? Laboratory and field research indicates that individuals who have specific and *challenging* goals are those who perform best. Obviously the probability of success in achieving a goal influences the strength of the employee's motivation. What is interesting is that goals which are seen as "sure things" are as unmotivating as those which are seen as impossible. The best goals—the ones which really inspire quality performance—are those which are seen as difficult and challenging but attainable. As we have seen in the McGregor section of Chapter 2, people do like to be challenged or to put it another way, to avoid boredom. But they also need to know that the difficult job is manageable. An overly difficult goal is as sabotaging as an overly easy one; indeed, people with a history of failure are particularly prone to set unachievable goals.

Whatever the goal turns out to be, it must be agreed upon by both parties. There must be ownership in the *process*, whether the goal is actually set by the boss or by the employee. When workers feel that they are actively participating in the setting of their own goals—even if the goals are first proposed by the employer—they are much more solidly motivated to perform with distinction than if they feel that they are merely being told what to do. Adults appreciate being treated as such. In particular, people tend to be highly motivated when they participate in the means for achieving an objective. This participation presupposes a manager who is willing to tell subordinates about the actual value of their performance improvement. The secretary who participates in determining *how* to get reports in on time needs to know *why* the promptness is important.

GOLF AND GOAL SETTING

An instructive analogy concerning the importance of goals and feedback is provided by the game of golf. Why are so many people motivated to play golf—to knock a tiny ball around a field? While the answer may seem to be "exercise," "the social element," or "the competition," a bit of probing reveals more basic factors.

For one thing, there are a number of extraordinarily clear goals in the game: you know which pin you are shooting for; you know the par; you know your own typical score. In the clear goals lies the key to what we normally label "challenge." The goals give the golfer not only a challenge but a system of guidance, something clear to shoot at and measure previous performance against. Golf even provides, in the par, the *ideal* goal: one that is neither too easy nor too difficult. It is a game which seems custom-designed to fit principles of motivation.

Those who doubt this need only consider those situations in the game when they were forced to hit a blind shot. Were the entire game a series of blind shots, it would rapidly lose its charm. Without pins, pars, scorecards—in other words, without goals—golf would be as absurd as it seems. In golf, as in work, goals influence motivation and performance.

The same analogy applies for feedback. Indeed, golf provides a textbook case for the efficacy of feedback. According to basic principles of psychology, feedback serves both motivational and instructional purposes: practice and repetition create neither excellence nor interest without a knowledge of what one is going for and how one is doing. For this feedback to work, it must be immediate, direct, and related to a goal. This is where the golf analogy comes into play: golf provides continual feedback—after every shot, every hole, and every round. Furthermore, the feedback that is delivered is direct, immediate, and connected to a concrete goal.

Again, the skeptic need only consider the alternative. How long would anyone play the game if he or she couldn't see where shots went, did not know the par or pin placements, and could not keep score? It is precisely these elements which motivate people to struggle to improve themselves in this arduous game when they could just as easily go to a movie or watch tv. Goals and feedback motivate people, in both golf and work.

We might point out here that the need for immediate, direct, goal-related feedback is similar to the need for these same elements in giving positive reinforcement. (See Chapter 5.) For our purpose, feedback, when it is positive, is virtually synonymous with positive reinforcement. We might also add that positive feedback should be given at every appropriate opportunity. Praise, when deserved and when given in a precise manner, is powerful motivational material. It raises self-esteem and makes people want to perform well.

The careful reader of this book has noticed by now that many of these principles—the need for feedback, the need for positive reinforcement, the need for enhancing self-esteem—frequently overlap because they are closely interrelated. In the golf analogy, for example, there is a final point which relates to a crucial aspect of goals and feedback. As we have seen, people are more motivated to perform when they perceive that they are treated as adults and are allowed to participate in setting their own goals. One of the keys to the popularity of golf is the requirement of judgment, discretion, and self-control that is built into the game. The golfer must continually choose clubs, judge distances, speculate on greens, judge wind, choose appropriate strategies, and set goals. For all these, the golfer is accountable for the consequences. If golf required no judgment, decisions, or self-direction, it would utterly lose its point.

For many disgruntled workers, their jobs lost their point long ago. To see why, let us speculate on what golf would be like if a typical manager were in charge of the game. First of all, the boss would undoubtedly rule that it's upper management's job to know goals and monitor performance. No self-respecting authoritarian manager would trust workers with important information such as pars, distances, and pin placements. After all, workers are basically lazy: they would probably try to peg par at an easier level. Our manager would probably decide not to set clear goals but instead to train supervisors in how to exhort

workers to "keep swinging, do your best, play a good game."
If workers get uppity and ask what they are shooting at, tell
them that's management's concern—tell them to just keep
swinging.

The same depressing logic would apply to feedback. After
all, our manager would reason, if employees discover that they
are doing well, they might revert to their normal laziness and
become complacent—or they might demand a pay increase. On
the other hand, if they discover that they're not doing well, they
might go to pieces. The best thing to do, our manager would
say, is to forget about direct feedback and design a rating form
to be administered once a year. Feedback once a year is plenty.
All we need to do is get supervisors to take notes throughout
the year on how well people played various holes, on how they
looked, on whether or not their golf shoes were polished. Also,
we don't want to get these golfers confused: give each one a
single club to swing and hire some specialists—green readers,
wind specialists, scorekeepers, scorekeeper checkers, and aud-
itors of scorekeeper checkers.

This nightmare scenario—in which the entire motivational
point of golf is "managed" out of existence—is not at all far-
fetched. If we imagine a game of golf in which the players don't
know pars, can't see the pins, don't have the vaguest idea of
how they're doing except once a year, swing only one club, and
have all judgment and participation removed from their power,
we are in fact visualizing a paradigm of many work environments. One is just as deadly as the other: golf without pins,
pars, and scores is like work without goals, feedback, and participation. In both cases we have low motivation and sluggish
performance. Eventually we have absenteeism, alienation, and
quitting; the golfer eventually goes over to bowling.

CONDITIONS FOR GOAL SETTING

One point we might clarify is that setting goals and maintaining
communication are the essential priorities. Although we recommend participation as well, we recognize that in some situations assigned goals may be appropriate. It doesn't matter so
much *how* a goal is set as *that* a goal is set. Research indicates

that participatory goal setting works best in some instances and assigned goal setting in others—and that *both* work *substantially* better than telling employees to "do your best." The participatory method is superior to the assigned method, however, to the extent that it leads to the setting of higher goals. Workers in participative situations often insist on setting very high goals regardless of whether or not they attained their goals the previous week. Even workers with limited education (such as a recently researched logging crew in the South) are likely to set dramatically higher goals when they participate in the process. These seem to be significant, healthy signals, and we recommend participation in goal setting whenever it is feasible.

We keep stressing in this book that nothing succeeds like success and nothing fails like failure. This is particularly true in the case of goal setting. Supervisors should continually keep in mind that they can make telling contributions to the final products by building the employees' confidence so that they can accomplish the goals. This involves not just being "nice" but being direct and honest. For the process to work, the employees must trust the supervisors. If the employees feel that they have been one-upped or that the goals are just another means of exploitation, they may resist or subvert the goals.

Even workers who are reasonably paid may feel that management is using goals to put something over on them. This suspicion can be avoided if management is careful to be clear and supportive. Once goals have been worked out and are clear to everyone (whether formulated in a participative or assigned manner), it is the supervisor's job to provide support, to encourage a feeling of pride and self-esteem, to make the workers believe that they are capable of meeting challenging goals. If the goals are indeed met, the feeling of pride in achievement will reinforce the acceptance of future goals. As we have seen, the supervisor can use positive reinforcements to ensure that this process works.

GOAL SETTING, SELF-ESTEEM, AND PRODUCTIVITY

It is important for management to keep in mind that goal setting and follow-up significantly increase the rate of production. According to research summarized by Latham and Locke

(1979), a programmatic use of goal setting and feedback raises the level of production by an average of 19 percent. Absenteeism is substantially lower in companies that set challenging, specific, attainable goals than in companies which spout vague clichés to their employees such as "do your best." Goal setting and regular communication increase the challenge of a job, make it clear to workers precisely what they are expected to do, and deliver a sense of pride and achievement—all of which translate into higher production.

Yet organizational behavior specialists have met with resistance from many of the managers with whom they raise the issue. As we have seen continually in this book, managers tend to go for theories which are indirect or fancy or seemingly complex—which are, in a word, manipulative. Latham and Locke report that many managers resist goal setting precisely because it is so simple and direct. Surely, these managers reason, something fancier is needed. Yet research has demonstrated that the straightforward, clear approach is the one that works. At the other extreme, Latham and Locke report that often managers sneer at the idea on the grounds that it's so simple that everyone, including themselves, knows and practices it anyway. Yet when workers are approached after goal setting is introduced, they invariably state that never before had they known what their supervisors expected of them.

We urge managers and supervisors who have never consciously instituted a program of goal setting and two-way communication *not* to assume that these are in place. Rather, assume that the opposite is the case. According to the American Management Association study referred to at the beginning of this chapter, your workers probably have only the vaguest notion of what they're doing or how they're doing. The need to set solid goals and maintain communication may well be an urgent priority.

FACTORS TO CONSIDER WHEN SETTING GOALS

1. *Measurement.* How will the performance be measured?

2. *Criteria.* Would everyone agree that the performance level was or was not met?

3. *Level of difficulty.* Set goals that are difficult but attainable to increase the challenge of the job.

4. *Statement of goal.* Goals can be expressed in terms of:

   Accuracy   Quality
   Timeliness   Rate
   Completeness   Cost
                      Rating scales

5. *Participative Goal Setting.* Research indicates that the actual setting of a goal is more important than how the goal is set. Although participative goal setting has proved superior to assigned goal setting to the degree that it leads to the setting of higher goals, both participatory and assigned goal groups outperform groups with no set goals who are told "Do your best."

6. *Individual and group goals.* Goals can be developed for a work group as well as for an individual member of the work group. The goal of trainee, for example, may be different from the goal of a more experienced group member.

7. *Baseline.* It is important to establish how the individual and/or group is performing prior to the establishment of the goal. Evaluating movement toward the goal against an established reference point is motivating.

8. *Fast feedback.* It is motivating to be in close touch with how you are doing. It is only through fast feedback systems that performance can be corrected, if necessary. In situations where there is no established system of measurement, it is necessary to design one if goal setting is to be effective.

Goal-Setting Example

Vague desire: cost improvement
Specific goal:

I will **reduce** + **current payroll costs**
ACTION VERB   TARGETED AREA
+ **by 10 percent** + **by June 1** = **Goal**
MEASUREMENT   TARGET DATE

SKILL PRACTICE EXERCISE 9
Setting Goals

This exercise will help you develop skill in giving goal-oriented directives. Oommunications that conform to goal-setting criteria increase the chanoes of getting the type of result you want when you want it.

For each of the following vague directives, write a goal-oriented statement that could be substituted in a similar situation in your department.

1. *Supervisor to employee:* I'd like you to find out what you can do about the Grytex account.

   _____

   _____

   _____

2. *Manager to supervisor:* I've asked you to step in to discuss the personnel problem you've been having. Let's kick it around and see what comes out of it.

   _____

   _____

   _____

3. *Sales manager to salesperson:* You're not selling enough of the Beta product line. I want you to improve your sales in this area.

   _____

   _____

   _____

4. *Supervisor to employee:* This is really important; I want to talk to you about it. Let's get together soon.

   _____

   _____

   _____

5. *Supervisor to employee:* I'd like you to check out pump 12. I heard that it's acting up.

_____

_____

_____

6. *Supervisor to work group:* Our department just hasn't been operating efficiently enough. It must improve and improve soon.

_____

_____

Answers

1. I'd like you to find out what our gross sales were with the Grytex account for the previous two quarters, and I'd like the information for our next sales meeting on the 18th.

2. I've asked you to step in to discuss the turnover in your department. For the past 6 months it's been running between 25 and 30 percent. We have to cut it down to 15 percent by the end of next quarter. Let's focus our discussion on that for the next half hour.

3. According to your revenue plan you're supposed to increase your Beta product line sales by 33 percent in the first half of the year. There are only 2 months left, and you've only increased your sales by 10 percent. Let's talk about how you can get to 33 percent by the end of the next 60 days.

4. This is really important. I must talk to you about it. Let's meet tomorrow in my office at 2 o'clock.

5. I'd like you to check and see if pump 12 has a leak. Let me know by 3:00 this afternoon.

6. In the past 3 days our department has dropped 10 percent under our 97 percent standard. We must get operations back to the 97 percent level by the end of the week. I want to use this half-hour meeting to develop an action plan for achieving this.

PART THREE
MODELS FOR MOTIVATION

In the 1980 *Annual Review of Psychology,* Goldstein summarizes over 300 of the most important research articles on training that appeared during the 1970s. He concludes that "during this decade, the method that has generated the most excitement is clearly behavioral role modeling."

Many major corporations are teaching managers to successfully translate motivational theory into action through the process known as "behavior modeling." Modeling was originally confined to laboratory studies of social development in children. Applications of the process in industry in the early 1970s achieved behavior change that traditional management development training designs seldom approached. Hundreds of companies are now using the approach to teach skills in such areas as supervision, selling, sales management, interviewing, and performance appraisal.

Six Basic Steps

The methodology is outwardly simple. Six basic steps are used to provide the participant with the new interpersonal skills and the confidence to apply the skills in specific on-the-job situations. (See Exhibit 3.)

1. Cognitive Presentation   The initial phase of the developmental process involves the presentation of a series of basic concepts about the key skills to be learned and the steps necessary to implement them in a problem situation. This process occurs in a typical lecture fashion and is designed to provide the con-

EXHIBIT 3 **Workshop model.**

ceptual base necessary to facilitate permanent behavior change. It is during this phase that the general principles covered in Part Two of this book are introduced through lecture, videotape, and workbook exercises.

2. Modeling In groups of six to nine, supervisors view films or videotapes in which a model supervisor is shown effectively dealing with an employee in an effort to improve or maintain the subordinate's performance (or, the supervisors see a salesperson interacting with a customer, or an interviewer interviewing an applicant, etc.). Each film presents an 8- to 10-minute demonstration of specific action steps. Instead of making a broad generalization, the model shows at least one effective way of dealing with the situation. Step-by-step guidelines are provided, and the film or videotape shows action involving real life problems with which the participants can immediately identify, not hypothetical situations.

Goldstein and Sorcher (1974) point out that trainees will more readily identify with the person to be imitated (the model) if this individual exhibits a great deal of competence or expertise, is in a high-status position, controls resources desired by the observer, and is rewarded. Field testing has shown that supervisor-trainees identify best with actual company supervisors and employees filmed or taped in familiar surroundings as opposed to professional actors in unrelated work environments. In addition, by having each behavior model introduced by a company executive, top management becomes directly associated with the process, and the supervisor-trainees are more motivated to identify with the behavior presented.

3. Behavior Rehearsal Trainees participate in intensive practice and rehearsal of the behavior demonstrated by the models. In fact, the greatest percentage of the training time is spent in skill practice sessions. Most theory-based supervisory training does not provide the participants with specific information about *what* to do and also falls short in permitting them to learn *how* to do it. Behavior rehearsal, or structured role playing, allows the trainees to practice a new behavior pattern in increasingly difficult situations. Supervisors thus develop confidence in its use before they are back on the job and are expected to use it.

4. Feedback and Reinforcement Praise, approval, encouragement, and attention are all examples of social reinforcers that a trainee receives from the trainer and other trainees as his or her behavior increasingly resembles that of the model. But at no time is the trainee instructed to use only the behavior being learned when handling the situation being depicted. Each pattern is represented as an alternative that should be considered and added to the supervisor's behavioral repertoire, since research indicates that a key ingredient of effective supervisory behavior is flexibility: the ability to choose a way to successfully cope with a given situation. The trainee receives immediate feedback on how successfully the behavior is being used and at what point it should be transferred to the job. A supervisor's confidence in his or her ability to use the new behavior is built through practice and positive reinforcement in the classroom setting. Videotaping the behavior rehearsals effectively aids the feedback and reinforcement processes.

5. Transferring Training to the Job The principles of transfer enhancement are emphasized throughout the training period. For example:

> The training groups are kept relatively small (no more than nine in a group).
>
> In addition to specific behaviors, the general prin-

ciples of motivation are practiced, and the inter-personal skills taught are determined by the needs of the company. Eventually, participants are able to apply the general principles to new situations that were never modeled.

And finally, between classes, the participating supervisors are assigned homework designed to help them transfer to their jobs the behavior practiced during the training sessions. At the start of each training period, the participants describe, discuss, and demonstrate their experiences in applying behavior routines learned previously. This permits further shaping and reinforcement of the training for application on the job.

6. Management Reinforcement Managers of the supervisor-trainees are trained in reinforcement techniques and maintain responsibility for coaching, counseling, and reinforcing the supervisors as they use the newly learned skills.

Practice and Application of Technique

It should be recognized by the reader that while there are overwhelmingly positive results regarding behavior change and the observation of a model, this is only one part of a system of learning. Goldstein and Sorcher point out that "modeling alone is insufficient because, though it yields many positive effects, they are often not enduring effects." The value of rehearsal, feedback, and the rapid transfer of newly learned skills to the job should not be underestimated.

By reading the modeling scenarios and dialogs in the following chapters you can learn *what* to do. However, it will only be through practice and application on the job that you can convert this knowledge into skill. The modeling scenarios and dialogs are clearly a starting point.

8

MOTIVATING AN EMPLOYEE WHO IS HAVING A PERFORMANCE PROBLEM

Typically, the greater the time between an employee's performance problem and the supervisor's reaction, the worse the performance problem will become and the less effective will be the supervisor's intervention. As was discussed in the chapter on reinforcement techniques, behavior is largely a function of its consequences. Unsatisfactory performance that is ignored may be viewed as rewarding by some employees, and those behaviors that are rewarded tend to occur again. It should also be remembered that the longer a behavior pattern has been rewarded, the more difficult it is to modify. It is seldom too soon to consult with an employee who is experiencing a performance problem. Looking the other way, wishing it away and paying little or no attention to it increases the chances that it will become chronic.

Bringing a performance problem to an employee's attention can easily generate a defensive reaction, even when the focus is kept on performance and behavior rather than on personality and attitude. However, defensiveness will increase the more the conversation drifts toward an analysis of the employee's personality and motivation. Such conversations provoke the employee to protect his or her self-esteem through mechanisms such as denial, rationalization, passivity, and aggression. In productive discussions of performance problems, the focus is kept on the problem, not on the employee, and most of the time is spent talking about the future and the solution, as opposed to the past and cause.

The methodology described here has not been designed for the employee who is a chronic poor performer. The behavior pattern of the chronic poor performer may be so well established that it is no longer subject to being modified through the means provided by the work environment. In addition, it is not unusual to find that the problem underlying chronic poor performance concerns aptitude rather than motivation. Effective motivational skills will not substitute or significantly compensate for a faulty selection system. The principles and techniques that are the focus of this book are based on the assumption that the employee possesses the minimum aptitudes necessary to perform the work. Here, the term "aptitude" incorporates ability factors (e.g., mental ability, communication skills, and mechanical aptitude) and personality factors (e.g., emotional stamina, energy level, confidence, and self-sufficiency). Different jobs call for different aptitudes, and therefore the first and perhaps most critical step in motivating an employee is selecting the "right" employee to begin with. The "right" employee has aptitudes that are compatible with the work he or she is expected to perform.

The manager's ability to effectively analyze performance problems also influences the chances of a successful resolution. Mager's performance analysis design is an analytical problem-solving sequence that can be readily incorporated into the interpersonal skills framework we have outlined.

Mager (1970) defines a performance problem as a discrepancy between someone's actual performance and the desired performance. Once the discrepancy is identified, its importance should be considered. If the discrepancy is judged to be unimportant, it should be ignored. If the discrepancy is important, the manager should determine whether it is due to a skill deficiency. If so, either formal training should be arranged to develop the skill, or practice sessions should be provided to revitalize a dormant skill. There are times when simple solutions such as changing a job or arranging for on-the-job training may be most appropriate. Overriding all of the above is always the question "Does the employee have the aptitudes for the work itself?" If the answer is "no," then only a move to a job that is compatible with the aptitudes the employee possesses is appropriate.

If it is determined that the performance problem is not due to a skill deficiency, then the manager can consider the consequences surrounding the desired performance. The chapter on reinforcement techniques should be referred to; it may be found that the effective performance is either being punished or being ignored. For the desired performance to be maintained, it must lead to favorable consequences.

ACTION STEPS: PERFORMANCE PROBLEM

In the model you are about to read, the manager is able to clearly define the problem, deal with defensive feelings, and motivate the employee to improve by relying on the general principles and by following these action steps:

1. *Focus on the performance problem, not the employee.* This action step calls for the omission of any reference to the employee's personality or attitude. The focus should be on a specific performance or behavior that is not meeting standards. It should be made clear that the performance problem is not negotiable and must be resolved.

2. *Ask for the employee's help in solving the problem, and discuss both your ideas and the employee's ideas on how to solve it.* The more ownership a person has in the solution to a problem, the more the solution is valued. In addition, the person with the problem often has the best ideas for its solution. It is therefore appropriate for the supervisor to refrain from offering solutions to problems until the employee has offered solutions. In order to increase the chances that the person with the problem will suggest ideas for its solution, the supervisor should ask for ideas in an open-ended way. That is, the question should be phrased so that the response cannot be "yes" or "no." "What ideas do you have?" or "Tell me your ideas for resolving the problem" are far more effective than "Do you have any

ideas?" It is only after the employee has offered ideas and suggestions that the supervisor should offer some.

3. *Come to an agreement on and write down the steps to be taken by each of you.* Committing an action plan to paper increases the chances of implementation. Recording the employee's ideas is also a way to enhance self-esteem. If any ideas are to be rejected, it is essential to provide a full explanation as to *why* the ideas or proposed solution is inappropriate.

4. *Express your confidence in the employee's ability to correct the problem.* If the supervisor cites some previous problem that the employee corrected, the expression of confidence takes on greater authenticity. Keep in mind the power of the self-fulfilling prophecy: that which is prophesied is more likely to come true than not. Supervisors who convey doubt and suspicion about problems being resolved increase the chances that the problems will continue.

5. *Set a follow-up date.* By way of further reinforcing the fact that the resolution of the problem is not negotiable, a specific date and time should be set for reviewing the problem.

   Both the employee and the supervisor should be committed to the specific actions that will be taken between the time of the initial decision and the follow-up date.

6. *Praise the employee at the first sign of improvement in job performance.* Many supervisors either ignore improved performance on the premise that, after all, that's what the employee is being paid for or wait for the problem to be totally resolved before offering positive reinforcement. This action step calls for the shaping of behavior by focusing on the smallest improvement and building from there. The praise must be specific, since generalities will do little to influence a given behavioral area.

ACTION STEP IMPLEMENTATION

SCENARIO BACKGROUND *Jim is a top-level technician in a high-technology R&D facility. Dave, his supervisor, is increasingly concerned about the lateness of an important report for one of the operating divisions. He spoke to Jim once before about the problem, but now that the report is 2 months late, he has decided to have a formal sit-down discussion with Jim and will be following the action steps. He recognized Jim as one of his most effective technicians, but this problem must be resolved.*

SUPERVISOR:

(Action Step 1) Jim, I have been reviewing the section action items for this month, and I am very concerned about one in particular which deals with the Project 3 report. We had a commitment to the division to submit that report at the first of last month. As you know, we discussed this report at the end of last month, and you indicated that you would have the report completed by now. The report is now 2 months late. If we delay any longer in getting that report out, I am afraid we are going to lose the train of thought and the data that we accumulated in the project. If we are going to maintain our section productivity, we have got to get that report out by the end of the week. If we expect the division to support us next year with additional projects, we have got to show that we can complete the obligations that we have agreed to take on. I fully expect that within the next day or so I am going to get a phone call from the division asking where that report is.

(Action Step 2) Jim, I need your help on this. What I would really like is to find out what you can do to correct this situation and what you think can be done to make sure that we don't have problems with future reports.

EMPLOYEE: You know, Dave, I can't believe this! You know darn well that we are overloaded. Everybody in this section is overloaded. I already complied with the spirit of this by sending letters to these people every month. You've got copies of them. I am on the phone with them every other week. They know darn well what we have done, and as far as my current load is concerned, there is no place I can fit in a report. You'll have to take me off other projects. What is it that you want me to drop? Something has got to go. I have already taken plenty of work home, and my wife is mad at me now. If I bring more stuff home, there sure as hell is going to be a divorce.

SUPERVISOR:
(Active Listening) You think the need for this report has been satisfied by your communication with the division and that you are already overwhelmed by the work that you have to do and that you would be very hard-pressed to find the time to get this report out.

EMPLOYEE: Yes, right. You're absolutely right, Dave. This darn thing is an exercise in dullness—futile, futile. You know darn well that they won't read it anyway. People here just count papers. You know.

SUPERVISOR:
(Active Listening) It would seem to you that finishing the report at this time would mean that you were wasted on something which is almost useless.

EMPLOYEE: Yeah, futile, you know. The darn thing is not challenging. The job has been done. Basically, I am a problem solver—right? I'm not a report writer. Give me a problem. Watch my smoke. How about last week, that job, the semiconducting problem. I got on that one in a hurry—knocked it down. You were happy with that.

SUPERVISOR:
(Self-Esteem) You're right, Jim. I really depend on your help in critical situations. Your action on that job last week really got us out of a difficult situation.

EMPLOYEE: Thanks.

SUPERVISOR:
(Action Step 2) It helped us with the division. That's why I'm sure you can tell me what you can do to get that report out on time and what you can do to make sure that all your future reports get out on time as well.

EMPLOYEE: Dave, I can't see how I can clear anything away. I don't know how I can get it done in a week. I just don't know.

SUPERVISOR: Well, with all that you have done so far in the project in the way of getting data and writing progress reports, it is possible that what's left won't take a full week.

EMPLOYEE: Even if it only takes a minute, what divisional pocket do I put my hand in? Where's the money going to come from?

SUPERVISOR: Well, how long do you think it will take you?

EMPLOYEE: Well, I suppose I could do a pretty good job if I took the existing progress reports, sort of strung them together, did a scissors job, used some glue, and wrote some connecting paragraphs. I suppose I could do it in a couple of days.

SUPERVISOR: Great! It's Tuesday now, so can you have the report ready for me by noon on Friday?

EMPLOYEE: Paper is a very patient thing, Dave, but I have the real world to contend with. I've got phones. Is the secretary going to be free? I've got to juggle my schedule. I've got to get away—get away someplace.

SUPERVISOR:
(Action Step 3 and Reinforcement) Now these are good points. I'm glad you brought them up. In order to get away from the phones, why don't you go to the library, at least for 1 day. And I'll make sure that Jean is available no later than 2:00 on Thursday afternoon. She'll be available to you Thursday afternoon and Friday morning to get the information up to graphic arts.

EMPLOYEE: All right. That sounds reasonable enough.

SUPERVISOR:
(Action Step 2) Great. That solves our immediate problem. Now, what do you think you can do to get your reports on future projects out on time? For example, we have Project 4, with a report due at the end of next month.

EMPLOYEE: Ah, that's an easy one. I wish they were all that easy. I can have the contracts department set my budget at about $2000 and let me know what I've spent. This way I can allow enough funds and enough time to write the report. I can stop the project work and start writing the report right away.

SUPERVISOR: Well, when you start a project, you know when the report is going to be due. Asking the contracts department to add another flag shifts the responsibility from you to them. What do you think you can do—independent of the contracts department—to prevent reports on your projects from being late in the future?

EMPLOYEE: Well, I suppose I could use a desk calendar more effectively.

SUPERVISOR:
(Reinforcement) OK, that's a good idea. How would you do that?

EMPLOYEE: Well, every job has a due date. So, at the start of a job I could flip to the due date, turn back 2 weeks, and then over a period of 4 or 5 working days write myself a little note warning me that I have 2 weeks left, just in case I am on the road or something. You know, I suppose that would work.

SUPERVISOR:
(Reinforcement
and Action Step 2) Excellent! Anything else?

EMPLOYEE: No, I think that should do it. With your help, I can get this report out, and I can get to future ones as well, I think, by following these suggestions.

SUPERVISOR:
(Action Step 4) Good, I agree. And I am confident that you will be able to get this report to me by noon Friday and that you will also be able to meet your future report deadlines. Jim, your laboratory work is excellent, and I know that you don't want these administrative aspects of the job to get in your way.

EMPLOYEE: Fine, Dave, but I'm glad you realize that these reports are time-consuming and frustrating.

SUPERVISOR:
(Action Step 5) OK, let's follow this up next month—we'll see just how well your system is working. Perhaps the third Monday of next month—the 19th—would be a good time to get together. How does 9:30 sound to you?

EMPLOYEE: OK, 9:30 sounds fine.

(One day later.)

SUPERVISOR: Hi, Jim. How's the Project 3 report coming?

EMPLOYEE: Well, I'm on schedule for the Friday deadline, but I had to do a heck of a lot of juggling to get to it.

SUPERVISOR:
(Action Step 6)   I'm really glad to hear that you're on schedule for the Friday deadline. I notified the division that they'll have the information no later than Friday at 4:00. Again, Dave, thank you for moving right in on it and doing all that juggling.

EMPLOYEE: Well, that's OK.

SUPERVISOR: How about the desk calendar?

EMPLOYEE: It's on my desk, and I'm using it. I know that the reports are important. They'll be coming through on schedule.

SUPERVISOR:
(Action Step 6)   I know they will, Dave. Thanks again. I'm looking forward to reviewing your calendar system with you on the 19th.

SUMMARY

Despite the potentially touchy nature of the situation, the supervisor kept the focus on the problem rather than on the employee. It was the employee's late report that was dealt with and not his personality or attitude.

This supervisor pressed for ideas from the employee. He encouraged the employee to be the originator of his behavior, since he is likely to place the highest value on his own ideas. The supervisor asked the employee to suggest ideas for correcting the problem before he offered his.

In several instances the supervisor was able to defuse emotions and maintain productive communication by actively listening to the employee. He was able to pick up and accurately respond to the employee's feelings. That also contributed to maintaining the employee's self-esteem, as did the manager's willingness to point out those aspects of the employee's performance that were above average.

It should also be noted that the supervisor immediately reinforced all productive comments, clearly established an expectation that the problem could be corrected, positively reinforced early signs of improvement. At no point did the supervisor compromise productivity in order to achieve a human relations end. This approach places maximum emphasis on *both* a concern for people and a concern for productivity.

9

MAINTAINING
DESIRED PERFORMANCE

Learning theory tells us that when a performance is not followed at least periodically by an event or consequence considered favorable by the performer, the chances are increased that performance will drop. The more rewarding the consequences of performance are, the more likely it is that the performance will continue and strengthen.

Many supervisors see their job as one of intervening when things go wrong. They are often unaware of the fact that there are a great many "right" things happening every day that are going unnoticed and being taken for granted. The "thats what they're being paid for" attitude takes desired performance for granted and is often a first step in the development of a performance problem. Effective supervisors avoid only paying attention to performance extremes. Performance problems often become chronic because they are not addressed in their early stages and the employee who is meeting most standards and even surpassing some is taken for granted. If supervisors address only performance extremes (poor performance and extraordinary performance), they may unwittingly be causing average to above-average performance to deteriorate.

The supervisor in this chapter's model is preventing the erosion of desirable performance. She focuses on the specific aspect of above-standard performance, reinforces it, and begins a shaping process that will help to prevent a loss of motivation and that can encourage even higher levels of performance.

Notice that this interaction is purely positive. The supervisor keeps the focus on the area of performance that is above standard. If there were areas of performance deficiency, they would have been addressed at the type of session that is modeled in Chapter 8, the chapter on performance deficiency.

ACTION STEPS: MAINTAINING DESIRED PERFORMANCE

The following action steps are followed by the supervisor in achieving the objective of maintaining desired performance.

1. *Describe areas of performance that are above average, and explain why they deserve special recognition.* The praise that is being offered here must be directed toward specific behaviors and performance. It should not be some general statement of approval. While general compliments may give the employee a good feeling, they do not influence specific behaviors to the degree that targeted behavioral statements do. Furthermore, even targeted compliments have only partial reinforcing strength if an explanation as to why the behavior deserves praise is omitted. When reinforcing desired behavior it is typically safer to risk saying too much by way of explanation rather than too little. It is also true that when praise directed toward specific behavior and performance is accompanied by factual justification for the praise, the risk of sounding phony or insincere is eliminated.

2. *Ask what can be done to help the employee to maintain the above-standard performance.* A way to increase the chances of obtaining a thoughtful response to this question is to ask it in an open-ended way—so that the employee cannot respond with a "yes" or "no." It would be more effective to ask, "What can I do to help you maintain this performance?" than to ask, "Can I help you maintain this performance?" Employees typically make reasonable, worthwhile suggestions and requests in this circumstance. If, however, a request must be turned down, the supervisor need not hesitate

to do this as long as a full explanation is given as to why the request or suggestion cannot be acted upon. When given *all* the facts behind a decision, even an unpleasant one, employees typically respond in a reasonable and understanding way.

3. *Indicate exactly what action you will take.* Once the second action step is taken, you are automatically committed to this step. The supervisor should summarize precisely what will take place and when as a result of the interaction stimulated by the second action step. Vague comments and generalities do not motivate employees; they frequently reduce rather than strengthen the employees' trust in the supervisor and the commitment to performance.

4. *Express your personal appreciation, and indicate the company's awareness of the above-average performance.* When expressing personal appreciation the supervisor should use the pronoun "I," as opposed to the more general and rather vague "we." Some managers have been brought up on the notion that a manager should speak in terms of "we" when interacting with an employee, since this builds teamwork. In reality this is a small but important step in deferring responsibilities. After running into a stone wall, a football quarterback does not say, "We didn't execute the play effectively." Instead, he says, "You, left guard, didn't open the hole. I ran into a wall, and we're going to lose." The accurate use of "I," "we," "you," and "they" plays an important role in defining responsibilities in the organization.

The second part of this action step—indicating the company's awareness of the above-average performance—clearly signals the manager's role as a facilitator of the employee's growth and recognition within the organization. The manager both enhances the employee's self-esteem and offers solid reinforcement.

ACTION STEP IMPLEMENTATION

SCENARIO BACKGROUND   *Debbie is an account executive in charge of a sales territory for a business machine company. Debbie's area of specialization is word processing equipment. Carol, her sales manager, has noted several innovative actions that Debbie has taken and wants to see that her above-standard performance continues. She has asked Debbie to stop by her office.*

SALES MANAGER: Hi, Debbie. How are you doing today?

SALESPERSON: Fine, Carol. You asked to see me. Is there a problem with one of my accounts?

SALES MANAGER: Absolutely not! I just want you to come in for a few minutes. I want to tell you about some of the things that I like about the way you have been handling your accounts.

SALESPERSON: Oh, thank you.

SALES MANAGER:
(Action Step 1)   I was very impressed when I learned that you had joined the Parkersville Chamber of Commerce and that you have run ads in its quarterly magazine and written industry-oriented articles on our equipment for the magazine. I think that by doing that, you used your time extremely effectively and positioned yourself well with those twenty accounts and the executives in those accounts. As a result, your name is out now to those people—they have a clear image of our company, how you fit in, and how you and the company can work with them to address and solve some of their business problems. I think they see you as a resource that they can use in planning for the future. As a result of all this, I think, you've built some pretty good relationships with your accounts. I think you should be proud of that.

SALESPERSON: I am pleased, Carol. I really didn't expect my actions to be so effective. They were very well received by the industry too.

SALES MANAGER:
(Action Step 2) I would like to see you keep up your good work. What can I do to help you?

SALESPERSON: Well, Carol, now that you mention it, there are a couple of things that would be really helpful for me. One thing I would like is to have more control over selecting the people who work with my accounts. I think that I can be much more effective if I have people who are real producers handling the support functions. Let me tell you what happened with the one account in northern Virginia. I have been working on it, as you know, for over 3½ months, and the customer is expecting me to give him a proposal at the end of next month, but I'm not ready for it because the people who were supposed to get me the information just haven't done it yet. They have been sitting on the reports that I was supposed to get last week. When I call in and ask for the reports, they tell me that they are too busy. And when I do get a report, the information isn't complete; I have to do a lot of the research myself. I think that if I could have influence in selecting the people I need to work with my accounts, I could be a much more effective salesperson. I could approach a customer with greater confidence.

SALES MANAGER:
(Active Listening) You're frustrated and angry because you think you are wasting your selling time doing work that should be done by your support people.

SALESPERSON: That's it exactly, Carol. I believe I could improve my sales 20 percent if I could choose the support people.

SALES MANAGER: OK. Let's look at some of the possibilities. There are many people who are involved in this decision; we are not the only ones. However, in the long run, I think we can have an impact on the situation. In another month we will have a personnel planning meeting. What I would like from you, by the end of this week, is some suggestions that might help us to better match people and the markets. Then maybe we can attack some of these problems.

SALESPERSON: Great. I'll make a list of people who I think will really be effective in my market, and I'll give it to you on Friday.

SALES MANAGER:
(Action Step 2) What else can be done to help you?

SALESPERSON: Well, there is another thing, Carol. I am going to need your approval for a $2000 increase in my expense account this year. The regional chamber of commerce is sponsoring a convention in Miami, and I think it would be beneficial for me to attend it.

SALES MANAGER: Well, what kinds of results can you expect from using that money?

SALESPERSON: Well, last year I attended a 3-day meeting of the chamber, and I sold three systems as a result of the leads I got there. Most of the members are going to be at this convention, and I think I can really improve my sales volume.

SALES MANAGER: It sounds good to me. Let's talk more about it next Tuesday when we go over your account plans.

SALESPERSON: Fine.

SALES MANAGER:
(Self-Esteem) Let me make a note of that.

SALESPERSON: Since we are talking about help, there is something I would like you to do for me. You know Frank Martin, the general marketing manager of

Gentex. I'm going out there next week to talk to Gentex's president about a new system for that company. I would like to get some additional background information on the officers and executives before I go out there. Could you arrange for me to talk to him?

SALES MANAGER: Frank Martin indicated to me that he wants to work more closely with our company. I'm sure he would appreciate hearing from you directly. I'll give him a call and clear the way.

SALESPERSON: I'd really appreciate that.

SALES MANAGER: Good. Anything else?

SALESPERSON: Yes, there is one more thing. I really would like you to go out with me more often on some of my sales contracts. I am trying to improve my selling technique, and I think the feedback that you could give me would really be helpful.

SALES MANAGER: OK. When is your next appointment?

SALESPERSON: 2:00 tomorrow.

SALES MANAGER: You're on.

SALESPERSON: Great.

SALES MANAGER:
(Action Step 3) Let me summarize what we have agreed to do. On Friday you'll give me a list of support people that I can take to our personnel planning meeting next month.

SALESPERSON: Right.

SALES MANAGER: On Tuesday, in our account planning session, we will discuss that $2000 in more detail.

SALESPERSON: Sure.

SALES MANAGER: I'll give Frank Martin a ring today and let him know you'll be in touch this week.

SALESPERSON: Fine. That's going to help.

SALES MANAGER: And I'll see you at 2:00 tomorrow for our joint sales call.

SALESPERSON: 2:00 it is!

SALES MANAGER:

(Action Step 4) Before we leave today, I want to tell you that I really appreciate the job that you have been doing in positioning yourself with your accounts. And I think that others on the sales team can benefit from learning about some of your approaches, so I'm going to reserve some time for you to fill them in at our next sales meeting.

SALESPERSON: Thank you, Carol. It's nice to get a pat on the back sometimes. I am really excited about it, and I am looking forward to going out tomorrow on the sales call with you.

SALES MANAGER: So am I.

SUMMARY

This manager recognized the need to reinforce desired performance. While she is hard-pressed to find the time for this type of activity, she acknowledged the fact that it takes even more time to correct below-standard performance. Since, to a large extent, performance is a function of its consequences, the chances are increased that Debbie will continue to perform in an above-standard manner.

The manager avoided general compliments and offered praise about specific aspects of performance. Because of this, her comments are likely to be viewed as sincere and will have great reinforcing value in shaping specific behaviors.

In addition, the relationship between the manager and the employee has been strengthened. The employee's self-esteem has been enhanced because of legitimate accomplishment, and successes are more likely to happen in the future. Interactions of this type should take place at least as frequently as interactions that deal with performance deficiencies.

10
COUNSELING A DISSATISFIED EMPLOYEE

People are not always ready to openly deal with their feelings or able to immediately identify factors contributing to a loss of motivation. Consequently, a manager needs to be sensitive to signs of dissatisfaction and distress. As Levinson (1964) points out, all signs (symptoms) involve a change of behavior:

1. The person's usual manner may be overemphasized. A quiet person may become even more withdrawn. A well-ordered person may become overly concerned with details. An outgoing salesperson may increase his or her pace and be described as "hyper."

2. The person may become restless or agitated and have difficulty concentrating. Tense and jittery behavior may also be displayed.

3. Behavior changes that cause a person to act in ways that are contrary to what is typical for that person are usually a clear-cut sign of dissatisfaction and stress.

ACTION STEPS: COUNSELING A DISSATISFIED EMPLOYEE

In the situation that is being addressed in this chapter, the employee's performance has not fallen below standard. There is simply a behavior change that has been noted—one which the manager has decided to address. By doing so the manager is helping to prevent an eventual drop-off in performance.

The manager in this situation follows these action steps:

1. *In a supportive manner ask the employee to discuss*

his or her areas of dissatisfaction. This discussion should be held in a private location with a minimum of interruption. It should be made clear that you are interested in the employee as a person and that some observed change in behavior, as opposed to a performance deficiency, has prompted you to want to talk with the employee. Keep the focus on the behavior change by referring to the contrast between employee's typical behavior pattern and the one you have recently observed.

2. *Show understanding by actively listening.* Some supervisors will be tempted to offer immediate advice upon the first hint of a problem. This is often a mistake, since problems that are initially brought to the surface are often superficial and not necessarily the cause of the observed behavior change. It is in this circumstance that active listening can play a major role in helping the employee to get to the "real" issues.

3. *Discuss the causes of the dissatisfaction in addition to the symptoms.* The behavior change is the symptom, and this should be the springboard for locating the cause. Active listening will help to peel away superficial discussion. The manager should also search for the cause by exploring the events that were correlated with the change in behavior.

4. *Ask for the employee's suggestions as to how the causes of the dissatisfaction can be resolved, and offer yours.* Many managers feel compelled to have solutions to problems at their fingertips. In situations of dissatisfaction and distress the person with the problem often has constructive and worthwhile ideas for its resolution. At the very least the person with the problem should share in the responsibility for developing an action plan.

5. *Come to an agreement on the steps each of you can*

take. Vague commitments like "Well, let's look into it" and "Let's think about it" often intensify dissatisfaction and stress. Steps for resolving the problem should be articulated. Who will do what should be made clear and, when appropriate, committed to paper.

6. *Indicate that you value the employee and that you want to see the employee succeed.* An expression of confidence and support can help ensure a successful implementation of an agreed-upon action plan. Rather than saying "Well, let's see what will happen," it would be more motivating to say, "I think these are the kinds of ideas that can make a difference."

7. *Set a follow-up date.* It is critical to pin down a time for a second session. It confirms commitment.

The model deals with a problem that is work-related—one that the manager is equipped to deal with. Once a counseling atmosphere is established, you may realize that the cause of the problem is highly sensitive and involves off-the-job circumstances.

At this point it would be best to keep the focus on the way in which the problem may affect job performance rather than attempt to resolve the off-the-job personal problem. As a manager or supervisor, you are not a professional counselor or psychotherapist, and this limits the actions you can or should take. If you cannot resolve a problem within the means you have, then it is time to refer the person. A first step in a referral can involve the company's medical or personnel department.

Keep in mind that if it is determined that the problem is not work-related and is personal in nature, the employee may require professional help. At this point, you would indicate in a supportive manner that you are not really qualified to deal with the problem and, if possible, make an appropriate referral. In this type of situation, it is also appropriate to ask if there is anything that could be changed in the job to make it easier for the employee to work effectively while handling the personal problem.

ACTION STEP IMPLEMENTATION

SCENARIO BACKGROUND *Herb, Joan's supervisor, has noticed a change in Joan's behavior in the last 2 days. Instead of being her usual energetic self, Joan has been somewhat passive. She has been doing whatever she has been asked to do, but with a bit of reluctance. Although Joan is not demonstrating a performance deficiency, Herb has decided that something is bothering her and that he sould try to determine the cause of her dissatisfaction.*

SUPERVISOR: Joan, would you call Mr. Kane at Plaza Metal and let him know that his order will be arriving around noon tomorrow?

EMPLOYEE: OK, Herb. I'll do whatever you tell me.

SUPERVISOR: Fine, I'd appreciate it. When you get through with that, I would like to talk with you in my office for a minute, please. There is something I'd like to cover.

EMPLOYEE: Whatever you say, Herb.

(Later, in Herb's office.)

SUPERVISOR:
(Action Step 1) Joan, just a few minutes ago, when I asked you to call that customer, you said, "I'll do whatever you tell me." You seemed kind of, well, blah. It was so unlike you. It made me wonder whether something's bothering you.

EMPLOYEE: Well, nothing. Nothing is bothering me. Everything is fine.

SUPERVISOR:
(Action Step 1) That's funny, because I can't help thinking that something is on your mind. You haven't been smiling as much all morning. As a matter of fact, when Mary came over to you and asked you a

question about an order—she had some sort of question—I noticed that you couldn't help her. Usually you're quite willing to assist; you're usually quick to offer a suggestion or help. But this morning you just turned Mary down; you turned her off. She just walked away; she didn't know what to do. That's not like you, and I was just wondering what's wrong.

EMPLOYEE: Maybe that's Mary's problem. *(Pause.)* Well, we all have our days, I suppose. Maybe this is my day.

SUPERVISOR:
(Action Step 1) It seems to go a little bit beyond that. You know, you've been in the dumps the last few days. You just haven't been smiling as much. You look unhappy, as if something is bringing you down.

EMPLOYEE: I'm not aware of anything, Herb. I went to bed late last night; I watched the late movie, and then I didn't sleep well. Nothing, as far as I can see, Herb.

SUPERVISOR:
(Action Step 1) Well, it's just not like you. Are you sure it's not something here in the office, something at work, that's bothering you?

EMPLOYEE: Maybe—I guess the typing is getting heavier. *(Pause.)* I can't say it's just the typing; it seems to be a whole lot of little things, Herb. I can't pinpoint any one thing; everything just seems to have fallen down.

SUPERVISOR:
(Action Step 2) So, it's the amount of work you've been doing lately in addition to some other things that are getting to you.

EMPLOYEE: I never minded working—even working overtime. You make it sound like I don't want to work. I like to work, and I like to work for you, and I like our department. And I was under the impression, quite frankly, that you were happy with me too and that the quality of my work was all right. I had hopes of doing something better than what I'm doing now. It was fine to begin with and to learn, but now all of a sudden nothing is really worthwhile. You know, we just had a promotion in the department, and I lost out for some reason or another—I don't understand; I don't know why. I had hopes; I thought that the job was going to be mine; I had foreseen this opening quite a while ago. The typing and everything else was fun because I thought I was learning, so it was all worthwile. Now I feel that maybe I wasn't doing such a good job, that maybe you didn't like me all that well. I just don't think it's fair.

SUPERVISOR:
(Action Step 2) So, you're still disturbed about not getting promoted to the customer service correspondence job. Obviously, you thought you were qualified for it and that you deserved it, but since you din't get it, you're upset.

EMPLOYEE: Yes, I'm very upset about it. Now that you've brought it up and it's out in the open, I think that maybe it's a good idea to discuss it.

SUPERVISOR:
(Action Step 3) OK, why don't you tell me again.

EMPLOYEE: I felt that I was gradually learning that job, that I had the basic background from the little bit that I did with the customer service backup work. Whatever you asked of me, I tried to do the best that I could, and I thought you were happy with that. I know that Mary has more technical background than I do. So in that area she's better qualified, but then again I was so tied up with my other responsibilities that I couldn't get into these details. But you know that in time, Herb, there is no reason why I couldn't learn these things too. I feel that all my efforts in that area were wasted—it was all for nothing. I really wonder if you think that I am going to continue doing the same thing that I've been doing. Maybe, Herb, you can help me find something else, elsewhere.

SUPERVISOR:
(Self-Esteem) Joan, I certainly don't want to see that! You know, you must know, that I really rely on you to do a number of things in the department—not just the customer service work that you do, but all the special projects that I assign you—the special tasks, the things that come up during the course of the day, the forms coordination. You know I gave that to you about a month and a half ago. Since then there hasn't been one problem, not one form out of stock. Nobody has come to me saying that we have run out of certain forms, and we haven't had to stop processing orders because you've really done an excellent job with the forms.

(Action Step 4) I'm really interested, at this point, in your suggestions. What can I do for you to change the way you feel about your job?

EMPLOYEE: I don't know, Herb. I guess I had all my hopes on that one position. I cannot come up with any solution. I was hoping that maybe you could help me.

SUPERVISOR: OK. Well, when we first discussed the promotion, I said that you had been seriously considered for the position. I knew when we spoke previously that you weren't 100 percent convinced of why Mary was chosen for the promotion, but I really didn't think that you were this upset about it. You were seriously considered as a prime trainee for the customer service correspondence job. Your work with the forms coordination and your advertising responsibilities did not lay in the customer service area, although there are certain responsibilities there that are very similar. On the other hand, you did do an excellent job with the customer service backup work despite the fact that we didn't give you any formal training in that area. I think it would be worthwhile to review Mary's qualifications. She's been an order editor for a year and a half; she's been right in the mainstream of our order processing system. She has product knowledge that is related to all our divisions, something that we couldn't give you in your training program, something she acquired during the year and a half she's been an order editor. She knows all the promotions; she's very familiar with the nature of each business, of each division. She knows all the exceptions, and she knows how to handle them. In addition, she has an associate degree, and she's working toward her bachelor's degree. Well, all those things helped to determine that she was the person most qualified for the position.

(Action Step 4)   However, I'm still very concerned about you. I'd like to know what I can do or what we can do to renew your interest in your present position and provide you with opportunities for advancement.

EMPLOYEE: Well, if you say that I didn't get this last promotion because of a lack of technical knowledge, then maybe I could work where I could get more technical knowledge.

SUPERVISOR: OK. What you're saying is that you want to be more involved in the mainstream of order processing.

EMPLOYEE: Yes.

SUPERVISOR: As opposed to advancement through the secretarial lines?

EMPLOYEE: Definitely.

SUPERVISOR:
(Action Step 4) OK. How do you think we can accomplish this?

EMPLOYEE: Well, would it be possible to reassign some of the work that I am doing so that I can have more time to train in other areas? The form letters are time-consuming; I think that anybody could handle them. The distribution of memos and postings within the department and the dictaphone work could also be done by somebody else.

SUPERVISOR:
(Reinforcement
and Action Step 5) You've got a few good points here. Certainly, the form letters are time-consuming, and there is really not too much involved in handling them. I think we can delegate them to someone else in the department. The distribution of memos and postings throughout the department can also be delegated, and that will save you some time too. However, I would be very hesitant to delegate the dictaphone work.

(Self-Esteem) The letters and memos that go to customers and the field sales force and the sales administration are important. I would be very reluctant to have someone else handle them because I'm confident that they are going to go out on time and be professionally done if you handle them. In addition, I don't think that responsibility for the supply cabinet should be delegated to anyone else. I tried in the past to have a person other than the one who is ordering the supplies maintain the cabinet and found that the plan became a fiasco. I would like you to keep these two areas, but I agree that a couple of the things you mentioned can be delegated to save you time: the form letters and the distribution of the copies within the department.

EMPLOYEE: Although you'll take some of my responsibilities away, I'm still basically going to continue doing the same work. The problem really won't change much.

SUPERVISOR:
(Self-Esteem) Well, I really need the excellent job that you do for me as my secretary. There are things here that I just couldn't do without, and you're the only person who can handle them.

EMPLOYEE: So, is there really no way for me to get ahead?

SUPERVISOR: There is a way. Why don't we take the time that we're going to make available for you and use it to work out a specific, systematic program for getting you involved in the technical aspects of order processing and other activities that will strengthen your chances for promotion.

EMPLOYEE: Well, that's fine. But even though you'll take a few jobs away from me and give me some training, will that be enough?

SUPERVISOR:
(Active Listening) You're afraid, then, that the program will just be a continuation of the way things have been going.

EMPLOYEE: Yes!

SUPERVISOR:
*(Action Steps 6
and 7)* Why don't we do this. There's a meeting in 10 minutes that I have to be at. Why don't we sit down again this afternoon at 2:30. We'll take an hour or whatever we need, and we'll map out this training program. We'll make it a formalized training program. We'll decide what skills you

need to develop—the skills that you haven't had the chance to develop because of the past situation. We'll determine which reports and systems you haven't had the chance to become familiar with. We'll do all we can to provide you with the opportunity to become a more qualified candidate, should a position open up in the future.

EMPLOYEE: It sounds very good to me, Herb.

SUPERVISOR: Good, I'm glad it does. I think it's the right approach. Do you have any other ideas? Do you think that there is anything else we can do?

EMPLOYEE: I can't think of anything else offhand, but if we work together on this problem, I think it can be resolved, and I'll feel a lot better about the future.

SUPERVISOR:
(Action Step 6) OK, I'm glad to hear that. If you do have any other suggestions, jot them down while you're at your desk and we'll discuss them when we meet this afternoon. I do value you, and I want you to succeed. I hope this program will give you the opportunity to develop the skills which will make you a more qualified candidate for a good position in the future.

EMPLOYEE: Well, I hope so too, Herb. I'm still a little disappointed about this last promotion, but I can better understand it, and I can see better things ahead.

SUMMARY

Through a 15 to 20-minute interaction, the supervisor prevented a potential performance problem from being realized. In this case the employee was not likely to bring the problem to the supervisor's attention. It is more likely that she would have become increasingly dissatisfied with her job and the company and that her performance would have deteriorated.

The supervisor skillfully pressed for causes of the dissatisfaction and advanced the discussion from "Nothing is bothering me" to "I didn't sleep well [last night]" to "The typing is getting heavier" to "Yes, I'm very upset about it [the promotion]."

The supervisor quickly responded to a noticeable change in the employee's behavior and dealt with it before it became a performance problem. He was supportive and skilled in active listening, and he knew the difference between symptoms and causes.

11
RESOLVING CONFLICT
BETWEEN EMPLOYEES

Supervisors who have attempted to resolve a conflict between two or more employees know how this type of interaction can easily get out of hand. It is not unusual to find many supervisors "looking the other way" rather than intervening and risking making matters worse. However, conflict between employees generally reduces efficiency and can have a detrimental effect on the entire work group. Unmanaged conflict is often contagious. Over time, its tendency to spread produces intragroup or intergroup polarization, or both. A win-lose mentality develops, and organizational objectives take second place to the defense of the ego. There is a loss of objectivity, and an increasing amount of energy is directed toward protecting one's position. The result of win-lose interactions is inevitably a loss of organizational effectiveness.

Since the type of conflict we are addressing is always interpersonal in nature, it indicates that interdependence is present to varying degrees. Properly managed conflict can actually have beneficial effects, and as Coser (1954) and Kuriloff (1972) have implied, conflict often acts as the catalyst for innovation to the benefit of organizational effectiveness. Whether employee conflict results in increased or decreased organizational effectiveness is very much a function of the skills of the third party.

Terminology adopted by Kuriloff is helpful in describing a two-step process for resolving conflict: (1) divergence and (2) convergence. The strategy of divergence and convergence includes identifying differences between the parties in conflict, working through them, and reconciling differences through convergence.

ACTION STEPS: RESOLVING
CONFLICT BETWEEN EMPLOYEES

In this chapter's model the supervisor is able to successfully apply the strategy by following these action steps:

1. *In private describe to the parties in conflict what you have seen and why it is of concern.* Privacy is necessary to ensure an open and frank discussion that is not interrupted. In describing what you have seen, the primary focus should be on behavior. Rather than saying "You're not cooperating with each other," it would be more effective to say, "I noticed that you're not relieving Mary when it's her break, and Mary, you're not relieving Betty when it's time for her to go on a break." In explaining "why it is of concern," a work-related reason should be given.

2. *Ask each of the employees to describe, without interruption by the other, the issues that divide them.* Each of the employees should describe in detail the issues that divide them. Each should be encouraged to ventilate his or her feelings. While this can increase the tension between the conflicting parties, it will provide an emotional release for the speaker. Here, the third party—you, the supervisor—must keep control of the discussion by disallowing any interruption during each party's description of the problem as he or she sees it.

3. *Actively listen to each employee's statement of the problem.* Active listening is an excellent mediating device. In active listening you take no position of your own. Nor do you offer any advice. By reflecting the feeling and content of each employee's message, at least three purposes will be served. You will be establishing yourself as a third party who truly listens and understands a point of view. You will be helping to capture the essence of the problem as each of the conflicting parties sees it, and by doing so you will be clarifying

the problem for both the speaker and the second party. You will also be helping to defuse the emotions of both parties, which is a key step in moving toward a more rational analysis of the conflict.

4. *Have each employee repeat the other employee's point of view, and have the other employee acknowledge the accuracy of the statement.* It is essential that each party understands the other. A statement like "I understand" is not sufficient evidence of truly comprehending the other party's point of view. Repeating how the other party views the problem ensures that the same issues are being addressed and also has a calming effect: the discussion becomes less emotional and more rational. The supervisor should remember to validate the accuracy of the recipient's statement of the problem through the speaker.

5. *Point out areas of similarity, such as interests and goals and how each employee depends on the other.* The convergence phase begins here. In all conflicts there are areas of common interest. The parties are apt to have similar needs, goals, and motives. The prospect of intentions being more readily realized through a joint effort should be stressed, as should the strengths and potential contributions of each party. This step provides the setting against which constructive action planning can take place.

6. *Ask each employee to make suggestions as to what can be done to resolve the situation.* Well-defined positive actions should be developed by the parties in conflict rather than by the supervisor. It is essential that suggestions have a focus on behavior. "I'll do my best not to argue" would not qualify as a positive, well-defined action.

7. *Come to an agreement on the steps each will take, and set a follow-up date.* The supervisor should write down viable suggestions and at this point in the discussion

summarize each party's action plan. Asking each party to be committed to carrying out the action plan is also helpful. Establishing a follow-up date in the near future emphasizes the fact that the conflict must be resolved and that the supervisor will not be leaving loose ends. The resolution phase will occur more rapidly with a specific follow-up date than without one.

ACTION STEP IMPLEMENTATION

SCENARIO BACKGROUND *Joe is a machine adjuster; he repairs most production-type pieces of machinery. He is proficient at his job and has been at it for the past 5 years. Anne is a machine operator with 2 years of experience. She is a conscientious employee who typically meets or exceeds production standards. Anne has been working on one of the older machines for the last few weeks. Although management has adjusted her production schedule to take into account the repair time needed for her machine, she is proud of her production capabilities and upset about the downtime she's been experiencing. She is convinced that Joe is not giving his best to the repair of her machine. Joe is convinced that Anne is a chronic complainer who refuses to understand the difficulties of working with older equipment. Their supervisor has decided that their bickering must be dealt with, since it can hurt production and lower the morale of coworkers in the department.*

ANNE: Hey, Joe. You'd better come over and fix this machine again.

JOE: What's the matter with you now?

ANNE: I've had it with you! I wish you'd learn to fix a machine so it can run for more than 1 day without breaking down.

JOE: Didn't you see me doing my job on the machine?

ANNE: No, I didn't see you doing your job. I showed you that the labels had to be fixed because they were crooked, and what did you say? "I've done all I can."

JOE: Well, I spent a whole hour just getting the labels fixed up. You saw what I did, and now you're trying to tell me I didn't do my job.

ANNE: Right! That's exactly what I'm telling you.

JOE: Well, you don't know what you're talking about.

ANNE: I know what I'm talking about!

SUPERVISOR:
(Action Step 1) Hi, Joe. Hi, Anne. I'd like you both to take a break and meet with me in my work area. In the meantime, I'll have your stations covered.

(In the privacy of the supervisor's work area.)

SUPERVISOR: Joe, Anne, you both seem to be having some difficulty. For the last few days I've noticed that the two of you have not been getting along.

(Focusing on Behavior) You've been arguing; your voices have been raised; you look the other way when you pass each other. All of this is of concern to me. The other day when I asked if there was a problem, you both said that things were under control, that everything was OK. Now, I see you're still going at one another, hot and heavy. You're both aware of the fact that our operation depends on teamwork to achieve our production goals. Let's try to get to the bottom of your differences so that we can iron them out once and for all.

(Action Step 2) There are two sides to every story. I would like each of you to tell how you see the problem, one at a time, without interruption. Who would like to go first?

JOE: I'll go. Yesterday she called me a couple of times, and I went over and fixed the machine. She was getting ridiculous and kept saying that I didn't know what I was doing.

ANNE: Right, and that was the case.

SUPERVISOR: Anne, let's stick to the ground rules. No interruptions while the other party is talking. OK?

ANNE: Well, OK.

SUPERVISOR: Joe, why don't you continue.

JOE: Now, I fixed everything that I could on the machine because I have a lot of experience, more than she has. She's only been here 2 years, and she is trying to tell me what to do. I did everything I could with the components we have for a machine that's old. We have to do the best we can with what we have. She doesn't understand that, and she keeps telling me that the machine is not running well.

SUPERVISOR:
(Action Step 3) Joe, you feel that you're caught in the middle. You are doing the best you can, fixing and re-fixing Anne's machine along with everything else you have to do on the floor, and you're really at your wit's end trying to figure out what else can be done.

JOE: Well, yes. I went in five times yesterday, and I'm tired of her. I fixed the pump, and I fixed all the valves on the machine and the chain and everything else, and she keeps telling me that the machine is not right. Now, what does she want? I did everything I could on the machine.

SUPERVISOR:
(Action Step 2) Anne, thanks for giving Joe a chance to talk about the problem as he sees it. Why don't you tell us how you see it. Joe, you'll have a chance to react, but remember not to interrupt Anne.

ANNE: Yesterday, I called five times. The labels are still crooked. Every time I call him, he is busy on another line. You have to wait for him every time.

JOE: What are you talking about?

SUPERVISOR: Joe, please. No interruptions.

ANNE: He says I'm not experienced. I'm experienced enough to see that a label isn't straight. He doesn't know what he is doing. Look at all the rejects I've got here. Who's going to get in trouble? Me. I want the labels straight and right! That's it!

SUPERVISOR:
(Action Step 3) You're really upset by the situation. You want to do a good job, and yet the condition of the machine is preventing you from doing as well as you would like.

ANNE: Yes, I'm upset!

SUPERVISOR:
(Action Step 3) You're really trying to meet your production goals. You keep getting frustrated by crooked labels, and you think that Joe isn't doing all that he can do.

ANNE: Right. I was so frustrated yesterday, I wanted to go home. He doesn't know how to fix the machine. I know what I'm doing, and he doesn't.

SUPERVISOR:
(Action Step 4) OK. Now, why don't you each repeat what you heard from the other. Anne, you go first. What was Joe's point of view?

ANNE: He said that he fixed the machine five times and that he has a lot of experience. He's saying that the machines are old, that components are hard to get, that he's busy working on a lot of other machines and caring for the lines, and that he doesn't know what else to do.

SUPERVISOR:
(Action Step 4) Is that right, Joe?

JOE: That's right; that's what I said.

SUPERVISOR:
(Action Step 4) All right. What was Anne's point of view?

JOE: Well, OK. She said that she was losing a lot of production and that she was getting a lot of downtime because of the machine stopping. She said that she's getting a lot of rejects. And she even said that I didn't know what I was doing.

SUPERVISOR:
(Action Step 4) Anne, is that correct?

ANNE: That's right.

SUPERVISOR:
(Action Step 5) Good, you seem to be aware of each other's point of view. I'm glad to see that you are both concerned about getting your jobs done the best way possible and that you're both interested in keeping our department's production up. It's also evident that you depend on each other and need each other to get your jobs done. Since you have all that in common, I'm sure that you can work together to solve the problem.

(Action Step 6) After all, you both have the same objective in mind. What suggestions do you have for resolving the situation between you?

ANNE: I can't think of anything.

SUPERVISOR:
(Action Step 6) Well, let's come up with some ideas. Let's put our heads together.

JOE: Well, what do you think?

ANNE: I don't know. Maybe we could slow the machine down a bit and see if that helps.

SUPERVISOR:
(Reinforcement) That's good, Anne. It's a constructive idea, and I'm sure that we can come up with some others.

JOE: Maybe I overlooked some of the problems yesterday. Maybe I could recheck the machine.

SUPERVISOR:
(Reinforcement) That's good, Joe. That's probably going to help too, and it's certainly a step in the right direction.

JOE: Well, I'm going to talk to my boss this morning and see what he can do. Maybe he could come up with a solution that I didn't think of yesterday.

SUPERVISOR:
(Reinforcement
and Action Step 6) That's another excellent idea! Any other suggestions?

ANNE: Well, I'll check the spools on the label machine and see if there are any defects.

SUPERVISOR:
(Reinforcement) Good idea.

JOE: Maybe there was a loose chain or the temperature wasn't right. I don't know—I guess I could check again. Who knows?

SUPERVISOR:
(Reinforcement) Good, Joe. That should help.

ANNE: Maybe we need to have test runs. Maybe he can come over every 10 minutes to check and make sure that everything is OK. Maybe he can do that for a couple of hours one morning.

SUPERVISOR:
(Reinforcement) Sounds to me like that's another idea worth trying.

JOE: Yes, I could do that tomorrow morning.

SUPERVISOR:
*(Reinforcement
and Action Step 6)* Well, I'm glad to hear these ideas. Do you have any more?

ANNE: I'll give him a break and stop saying that he doesn't know what he's doing.

SUPERVISOR:
(Action Step 7) I'm really glad you've both come up with these ideas. Let's see what we've agreed on. Anne, you're going to slow down the machine a bit to see if that helps. You'll also be checking the spools on the label machine for defects, and you'll be working with Joe on test runs tomorrow morning. Is that right?

ANNE: Yes, I'm in agreement with that.

SUPERVISOR: Fine. Oh yes, one more thing. You'll be holding back on telling Joe that he doesn't know what he's doing.

ANNE: I can do that.

SUPERVISOR:
*(Reinforcement
and Action Step 7)* I know you can, and I appreciate it. Joe, you've agreed to recheck the machine, discuss it with your boss, and work with Anne tomorrow morning on the test runs.

JOE: Yes, that's right. I'll do that.

SUPERVISOR:
*(Reinforcement
and Action Step 7)* I'm sure you will, Joe. You also agree that because she has 2 years of experience with the machine, Anne may be helpful in pointing out problems.

JOE: I guess so.

SUPERVISOR:
(Self-esteem
and Action Step 7) Joe, you're an experienced machine adjuster—and Anne, you're an expert operator. You both want to get the job done in the best possible way. I know that if you both work together, this problem with the machine will be licked. Let's get together again tomorrow, at the afternoon break, and you'll bring me up to date on how these ideas are working out. OK?

ANNE: Fine with me.

JOE: Me too.

SUMMARY

There are times when a conflict cannot be resolved in one meeting. In more complex situations a series of meetings may be called for. However, the same sequence—divergence and convergence—can be followed. It is essential for the conflicting parties to recognize that the inefficiencies and other work-related problems they are causing cannot continue. The prime role of the third party is that of a mediator who insists on a resolution of the problem but is basically nonevaluative in behavior.

The supervisor in this model enhanced the mediating role through active listening and kept the focus on behavior and problem solving rather than on personality and faultfinding. Emotions were ventilated in a controlled interaction, and perceptions were clarified. In this case, properly managed conflict had beneficial effects and was the catalyst for the kind of innovation that benefits the organization.

12

HANDLING FORMAL CORRECTIVE ACTION

Although behavior modeling and its application to supervisory skills training (SST) have achieved such concrete results as decreases in employee turnover, absenteeism, and grievances and direct productivity increases, misconceptions about the process and the skills being taught are commonplace. The primary purpose of this chapter is to demonstrate how our general principles and their derivative action steps can readily be utilized in a tough disciplinary action procedure in a unionized manufacturing plant.

In all work environments management should establish a "positive discipline" atmosphere in which employees willingly accept and abide by rules which they believe are fair and appropriate. Under such conditions, the work group will frequently exert social pressure on those who violate work rules, and there will be less need for formal corrective actions. Pressure from the work group itself to abide by work rules is strengthened by consistent evidence that all rules are being enforced. One of the quickest ways for a supervisor to lose the respect and cooperation of subordinates is to improve discipline in an arbitrary way. Inconsistent disciplinary action is one of the most disruptive and dysfunctional behaviors a supervisor can engage in.

Can disciplinary actions be made consistent with our general principles of motivation? We think so, through what Douglas McGregor called the "hot stove rule." This rule draws an analogy between touching a hot stove and experiencing discipline.

When you touch a hot stove, your discipline involves a warning and is immediate, consistent, and impersonal:

1. *Warning*—A typical sequence of penalties under "progressive" discipline is as follows:

   a. Oral warning

   b. Written warning

   c. Disciplinary layoff

   d. Discharge

   With reference to our hot stove analogy, if we envision a red-hot stove, we know what will happen if it is touched. The consequence of the action is evident.

2. *Immediate*—The burn would be immediate, and there would be no question of cause and effect. As we discussed in the chapter on reinforcement, the closer the consequence is to the behavior, the more it is associated with the behavior. A long delay between the infraction of a rule and the consequence disassociates the two events.

3. *Consistent*—Everyone who touches the stove is burned. As previously noted, there are few behaviors a supervisor can engage in that are more demoralizing and disruptive than inconsistent disciplinary action.

4. *Impersonal*—Individuals are burned not because of who they are but because they touched the stove. The supervisor must maintain a focus on behavior. As Argyris (1953) points out, "Discipline is most effective and has least negative effect on individuals, if the individual feels that his behavior at the particular moment is the only thing being criticized and not his total personality."

ACTION STEPS: HANDLING FORMAL CORRECTIVE ACTION

In this chapter's model the supervisor will be following these action steps:

1. *Define the problem in terms of a lack of improvement since the previous discussion.* Here the focus must be kept strictly on the infraction of the rule. Any mention of personality or attitude will cause the employee to become more defensive. The supervisor must enter into this discussion knowing all the facts.

2. *Ask for and actively listen to the employee's reason for the continued behavior.* The employee must have an opportunity to state his or her point of view. Don't ask for an excuse; instead, concentrate on the cause of the rule violation. Active listening will help to reduce the adversary relationship and is an early indication of the supervisor's effort to maintain a helping role while fairly administering appropriate disciplinary action.

3. *If disciplinary action is called for, indicate what action you must take and why.* Sometimes an open discussion with an employee will yield mitigating information that speaks against formal corrective action. However, if you have decided that disciplinary action is appropriate, explain precisely what impact the employee's behavior has had on the job and exactly what action you must take. It is insufficient to simply indicate that a rule has been broken. The problems caused by the rule infraction must be explained.

   A positive consequence of resolving the problem should also be outlined. This is a frequently omitted step, and its absence decreases motivation to resolve the problem. If the formal corrective action is a letter of reprimand, a method should be outlined as to how the letter can be removed after a period of time or how another letter indicating a resolution of the problem can be placed in the employee's personnel file.

4. *Agree on specific actions to be taken to solve the problem.* At this point there is a return to problem solving, and the conversation becomes future-oriented. It is important for the employee to be committed to the specific actions that will be taken to resolve the problem. A statement such as "I'll try my best" is not acceptable.

5. *Assure the employee of your interest in helping him or her to succeed, and express your continued confidence in the employee.* There should be no indication of having given up on the employee or that this is a beginning-of-the-end situation. The supervisor should indicate that the employee is valued. This is a continuation of the supervisor's helping role and belief in the employee's ability to work toward the goals of the organization.

6. *Set a follow-up date.* There should be no doubt in the employee's mind that there will be a follow-up. A date for review in the near future should be set. Setting dates for follow-up reviews helps to reinforce the importance of the problem.

7. *Positively reinforce any behavior change in the desired direction.* Here is a clear-cut example of where the shaping process should be utilized. Rather than wait for the first formal review session to positively reinforce improvement, the supervisor should be quick to offer praise at the very first sign of the problem being corrected.

ACTION STEP IMPLEMENTATION

SCENARIO BACKGROUND *Jim is a supervisor in a busy manufacturing plant that is unionized. One of his subordinates, John, has had a lateness and absenteeism problem. Two weeks ago Jim spoke to John about it, but since the verbal warning there have been additional occurrences. Jim has decided to take the next step in the progressive disciplinary action procedure: giving a written warning. John and his shop steward are meeting with him this morning.*

SUPERVISOR: *(Action Step 1)*	Well, fellows, I called you here to discuss John's lateness and absenteeism problem. John, I've really been concerned about this lately.
EMPLOYEE:	So?
SUPERVISOR:	Well, 2 weeks ago when I spoke to you about the ten occurrences of the problem, I gave you a verbal warning. Since then you've been late two times, once on Wednesday the 12th and once on Friday the 14th, and yesterday you were absent.
SHOP STEWARD:	How late was he?
SUPERVISOR:	Well, on Wednesday he came in at 8:12, and on Friday at 8:32.
SHOP STEWARD:	So what? He's not being paid for the time he missed. He was docked for that amount of time, and he probably had a good reason for being late.
SUPERVISOR: *(Action Step 2)*	Well, what are your reasons, John? Why haven't you been able to improve this situation?
EMPLOYEE:	Well, there was a bad accident on Route 420, a great big truck tie-up. That was on Wednesday. I rushed anyway and got here—what was it—only 12 minutes late. Damn it all—I should have gotten a compliment for coming in as early as I did.
SUPERVISOR: *(Active Listening)*	You feel that I'm being unfair, that you deserve better treatment than this.

EMPLOYEE: Certainly I don't deserve these points that you guys give out here.

SHOP STEWARD: We don't even recognize those points.

SUPERVISOR: Well, what about Friday? 8:32.

EMPLOYEE: Friday I had a flat tire. Do you remember how badly it was raining on Friday? I got wet when I took the lugs off; the jack slipped; I had a hard time with the spare tire—putting it on. After I finished changing the tire, I had to come in the house and change my clothes, and then I got here.

SHOP STEWARD: That's a conscientious employee!

SUPERVISOR:
(Self-Esteem and Action Step 1) You're right, Ron. John has been very conscientious in the past. I used to be able to rely on him, but not any more. His attendance problem has reached the point where it's affecting the efficiency of my whole department. Yesterday, for example, I thought he was going to be late again, so I held up a job, knowing that his skill in assembling the valve would be needed. But he didn't show up at all, so around noon I gave the job to Pete. I really ended up losing the whole damn day.

SHOP STEWARD: If he's so skilled that you had to hold a job up, then he should be getting more money. Remind me to write up a grievance when we get out of here.

SUPERVISOR: *(Ignores shop steward's response and looks at the employee.)*

EMPLOYEE: The reason why I was out and couldn't call was that the night before I drove almost 200 miles. The car broke down, and I had no change. So I couldn't call. I couldn't even call my wife! And when I did get to a phone, it was after 4:00 and you weren't here—you were gone.

SUPERVISOR:
(Active Listening)   Sounds like you were in a difficult situation.

EMPLOYEE: You bet I was!

SUPERVISOR:
*(Active Listening
and Action Step 3)*   You've been having a lot of trouble with your car and with traffic. I know that can be frustrating, but these things have been happening to you an awful lot lately—over and over again. If it were the first time, John, I wouldn't be so concerned. The last time we talked about this, you indicated that you'd be able to resolve the situation, but you haven't. So it looks like I'm going to have to give you this warning slip.

EMPLOYEE: I think you're being unfair! I don't deserve any written warning whatsoever!

SHOP STEWARD: Why are you picking on him now? Let me ask you a question. You asked him to improve his attendance. Has there been any improvement? As far as I can see, there has been.

SUPERVISOR: Well, I wish I could agree with you, Ron. John is too valuable an employee for me not to be upset with the thought of losing him.

EMPLOYEE: Losing me? Where am I going to go?

SHOP STEWARD: Losing him? We came here to discuss a minor problem of absenteeism, and now you're talking about losing him?

SUPERVISOR:
(Action Step 4)   Believe me, what I want most is to help John to do a good job. Now, I know you can do it, but we must work things out—we must solve the problem of your coming in late. If this pattern continues, you'll soon be facing time off and even indefinite suspension. I want to help you, but my hands are tied unless you help yourself first.

SHOP STEWARD: I don't understand you. You talk about helping the guy, and yet you're rewarding him with a warning slip!

SUPERVISOR:
(Reinforcement) Well, Ron, nothing would make me happier than to be able to write another letter in the future for John's file indicating that he solved his problem and that the situation is a thing of the past.

EMPLOYEE: You mean that this slip will be torn up then? Why not do it now?

SUPERVISOR:
(Reinforcement) No, no, John. I can't tear this thing up now. It's going to become part of your record, but so is any letter that I write in the future indicating that you've improved. That will also become part of your record.

SHOP STEWARD: We're not getting anywhere.

SUPERVISOR:
(Action Step 4) I think we are making some progress. John, how about some suggestions. Can I help? Is there something that I can do?

EMPLOYEE: No—obviously my car's the problem. And the traffic's terrible.

SUPERVISOR:
(Action Step 4) Yes, I know. I drive to work every day myself from the Westchester area. It's a long way, and there's a lot of traffic on 95. But what about a car pool? Perhaps I can arrange for you to. . . .

EMPLOYEE: *(Interrupting.)* No, I don't want that.

SUPERVISOR:
(Self-Esteem and Action Step 4) Well, John, what do you think you can do? I want you to succeed here, so I really need your help and ideas on how your attendance record can be improved.

EMPLOYEE: Suppose I get up earlier and try to beat the traffic.

SUPERVISOR:
(Reinforcement) I think that probably would make a big difference.

EMPLOYEE: If I can't make it, I'll call in.

SUPERVISOR:
*(Reinforcement
and Action Step 5)* Good, good. Well, I'm interested in helping you succeed on the job, John. I'm confident that you can solve this problem by doing the things you just mentioned. John, what other ideas do you have about how you can lick this?

EMPLOYEE: I can't think of anything else. I think that what I said is the answer.

SUPERVISOR: Fine, John. So you'll be getting up earlier to beat the traffic, and if you're going to be late or out, you'll call in.

EMPLOYEE: That's right; I can do that.

SUPERVISOR:
(Action Step 6) I know you can. Why don't we get together next Friday just for a few minutes, you and I, and see how things are going. OK?

EMPLOYEE: All right. That's fine with me.

SUPERVISOR: OK. Would you both like a copy of this report?

SHOP STEWARD: Oh, no. You can keep that! We don't want it.

SUPERVISOR: OK. This is part of his record, and I've got copies here. They are for your reference if you want them. OK, gentlemen. Thank you for your time.

SUMMARY

In this model the supervisor did not engage in "apologetic discipline" or in a personal bawling out. The supervisor was able to carry out an essential element of a performance improvement procedure while maintaining the self-esteem of the employee and following all the other general principles of SST. The supervisor's behavior was firm and constructive; the supervisor demonstrated a concern for productivity as well as a concern for people. The discipline was improved through a focus on behavior, and the employee was given a chance to express his point of view. After imposing the discipline the supervisor returned to the helping role and clearly conveyed a desire to do everything possible to help the employee succeed.

13
REDUCING RESISTANCE TO CHANGE

While most of us accept and even welcome changes in material things such as appliances and cars, we tend to resist changes in our interpersonal and job relations. Those changes tend to threaten the security of the orderly and familiar ways we have known in the past. There are also times when changes threaten our self-esteem as well.

The ability to introduce change with a minimum of resistance is a key supervisory skill, since we are living in an era of accelerating change. Resistance to change often shows itself in a variety of defensive reactions. Resistance can appear as an increase in absenteeism, resignations, and requests for a transfer and as lots of rationalization as to why the change will never work. One of the clearest signs of resistance is a series of emotional or irrational objections that clearly indicate that more deep-seated problems are involved. Typically it is not the change itself which causes the resistance but the meaning of the change for the people involved. For example, in this chapter's model the employees' self-esteem is at stake with the introduction of a woman in the traditionally male workplace. However, the supervisor anticipates the resistance and reduces it by following the action steps described below.

ACTION STEPS: REDUCING RESISTANCE TO CHANGE

1. *Clearly explain why a change is essential.* The more information people have about a change, the less the resistance. This information should include background factors that established the need for the change. In fact, it is often advisable to establish the need for the change before announcing the change itself.

2. *Explain the details of the change, and discuss how the change might affect the employees.* It is at this point that management should level with the employees. All information about the change itself should be brought to the surface. There should be no surprises once the change is instituted. Furthermore, an honest, straightforward statement about how the change may initially affect the employees should be made. Do not attempt to whitewash the change, for whitewashing typically erodes self-esteem and generates more, not less, resistance.

3. *Ask for and actively listen to the employees' feelings, questions, and concerns about the change.* Do not try to ram the change through by leaving little time for reactions. Two-way communication is essential, and an assertive request for reactions serves to stimulate such interaction. It is best to get all objections out in the open where they can be reacted to and perhaps overcome. If the supervisor does not provide a platform for venting objections, they will be voiced in the supervisor's absence and serve to reinforce resistance.

   By actively listening to all objections and complaints, the supervisor will prevent the establishment of a win-lose condition with the employees. Instead, a problem-solving model will be established that helps to generate cooperation.

4. *Ask for the employees' ideas on how the change can best be accomplished.* The more the employees participate in implementing the change, the less will be the resistance. Even though management's ideas about the change may work in theory, the employees typically have the know-how to make the change work in practice. Incorporating employee thinking into a change is another key means for reducing resistance.

5. *Make it clear that only with the employees' help and support will the change work and the objectives be*

accomplished. While it should be made clear that the change itself is not negotiable, it should also be understood that only with the full help and support of the employees, will the objectives of the change be realized. An expectation of full support should be established, and a specific commitment should be asked for.

6. *Follow up on the change, and praise the employees for their cooperation in accomplishing the change.* Changes become part of the system over time. It is up to the supervisor to make certain that resistance doesn't begin to build in the latter phases of a change. Follow-up is critical, as is reinforcement for making the change work. Reducing resistance to change is not a one-shot effort.

ACTION STEP IMPLEMENTATION

SCENARIO BACKGROUND *A supervisor in a plant where plastics and chemicals are manufactured has been told that a woman will be assigned to his all-male work group. A position has been open in the work group for 2 months, and the employees are eager to see it filled. While they are aware of the plant's strong commitment to affirmative action programs, they are not expecting this traditionally male position to be filled by a female.*

SUPERVISOR: *(On the phone.)* Yes, Patsy Miller on the 17th. OK, I'll expect her out here on the 17th then. OK, thanks for calling. *(Supervisor's work group is preparing to start a shift.)* Hey, fellows. Let's have a meeting over here for a few minutes. I've got some information to pass on

(Work group meets in a corner of the locker room.)

SUPERVISOR: As you fellows know, our group has needed extra help for some time now. Well, we finally got it.

WORK GROUP: Great! It's about time. Finally.

SUPERVISOR:
(Action Step 1) You're also aware that Ajax is committed to implementing the guidelines set forth by the Equal Employment Opportunity Commission and that therefore the company has an affirmative action program regarding the hiring of minorities and women. Actually, this has opened a new labor pool to us, and in order to take advantage of it we've also made a heavy commitment to training. What this combination means is that we can staff certain jobs faster. Well, Patsy Miller will be joining us on the 17.

(Action Step 2) She'll be starting as a mechanic's helper, and we'll be requiring her to do everything that's involved with the job. It may seem a bit awkward and unusual at first to have a woman in the group, but she's going to help us get our job done.

(Action Step 3) Now, what are your reactions? What kinds of questions or concerns do you have?

EMPLOYEE 1: I'll tell you one thing—my wife's not going to like this.

EMPLOYEE 2: Yeah, that's right. And what about the heavy equipment? How is she going to handle that?

EMPLOYEE 3: This is probably some kind of test or experiment put together by those women's lib people.

SUPERVISOR:
(Action Step 3) OK, you guys have plenty of concerns about how she's going to fit in and whether she'll be able to carry her own weight around here.

EMPLOYEE 4: Damn right! Sounds to me like we're going to have to work harder with her here than without her.

SUPERVISOR:
(Self-Esteem) I know that you guys have always cooperated with and helped new employees who have shown that they want to do their part of the job.

Well, she's going to have to do her job, and I can assure you that there will be no compromises.

EMPLOYEE 2: No compromises?

SUPERVISOR:
(Active Listening) Carl, you doubt that she'll have to live up to the same requirements the men have.

EMPLOYEE 2: You bet I do.

SUPERVISOR: Well, I can tell you this: I interviewed her, and I decided to say "OK" strictly because I think she can do the job. She has to work for a living, she's serious about needing a job, and she has lots of mechanical aptitude. She's a mature and stable person who I think is going to show up for work every day.

EMPLOYEE 1: She may need the job, but I bet we'll still have to carry her load. Other plants have female operators, and I've heard plenty of stories about them. We're going to have to do her work.

EMPLOYEE 2: Sure, that's what we think. And what's going to happen in an emergency situation—when she has to turn that big 8-inch valve we've got out there.

SUPERVISOR:
(Active Listening) So, there's also concern and doubt about her ability to do her part in a crisis.

EMPLOYEE 4: That's right! It's our lives we're talking about.

EMPLOYEE 2: You know, I heard about women working in plants during World War II. I heard that some of them were pretty good workers.

SUPERVISOR:
(Reinforcement) You know, I heard the same thing. I also heard that they had good safety records. At first the guys were against it, but they found out that lots of women could do the work just as well as a man could. You know, some safety surveys show that women perform more safely than men.

EMPLOYEE 1: It's people who do their share and work safely that I like to be with.

SUPERVISOR:
(Reinforcement) I feel exactly the same way, and I'm glad to hear you say that. You know that she's going to have to carry her own weight around here and meet all the safety requirements. OK, fellows. Patsy Miller is starting on the 17th.

(Action Step 4) What needs to be discussed and worked out is how to help her fit in smoothly. I need your help and ideas on this. What are your ideas?

EMPLOYEE 3: Does she have any experience in working with this type of equipment?

SUPERVISOR: Well, I can tell you that she has lots of mechanical aptitude, but she doesn't have experience with this particular type of equipment.

EMPLOYEE 3: Well, one thing that's going to have to be different is the training. You know, we are going to have to intensify our training a lot to make up for the fact that she hasn't worked with this equipment before. As far as I'm concerned, a woman just isn't as good with mechanics as a man.

EMPLOYEE 4: You've got to teach them everything from the ground up. Everything is going to have to be explained in great detail. There are things that we might take for granted, but a woman can't. Everything in the whole training program is going to have to be spelled out in detail.

EMPLOYEE 2: Yes, but there are a lot of men out there, and when they first came here, they didn't know anything about the work either.

SUPERVISOR:
(Reinforcement) That's it exactly. Just like new guys out there she's going to be trained, and if she doesn't pick it up the first time, she'll be retrained. You see, I'm confident that she can do this job.

EMPLOYEE 1: And what's going to happen if she can't?

SUPERVISOR: Well, you know the company policy. If she can't pick it up, she's going to have to leave and someone's going to replace her. However, I can tell you this—it's probably going to be another woman. We're going to have to learn to live with this, so let's make sure the training works.

EMPLOYEE 1: If we don't train Patsy, we are going to get another woman?

SUPERVISOR: That's a fact!

EMPLOYEE 2: Well, what job is she getting first?

SUPERVISOR: *(Action Step 4)* What are your ideas?

EMPLOYEE 3: Well, what did she do before?

SUPERVISOR: She was a homemaker.

EMPLOYEE 3: Oh, well. Then she probably doesn't know much about mechanical processes. I can't think of where to start her.

SUPERVISOR: *(Action Step 4)* What do the rest of you guys think?

EMPLOYEE 2: Why not "reaction"?

EMPLOYEE 3: That's too technical.

SUPERVISOR: Well, how about the bulk loading job? That's where we need help the most.

EMPLOYEE 3: Well, "reaction" is too technical, and bulk loading's too physical for her.

SUPERVISOR: If she can't do the job, she'll just have to leave. She's got to learn how to do the job, physical or otherwise.

EMPLOYEE 2: She might be able to learn the technical part, but the physical part's pretty heavy—she can't do it herself.

EMPLOYEE 1: Well, there are valves and hoses that I can't handle by myself, and I don't know many people who can.

SUPERVISOR:
(Reinforcement) That's exactly the case. I'm glad you can see that. When she runs into something like that, she's going to call for help.

EMPLOYEE 3: Who's going to be her trainer?

SUPERVISOR:
(Self-Esteem) Well, how about you, Armando? I think you're the most likely choice, since you're on the job right now and I think you're ready to be moved to another job. In fact, you have the most knowledge of the job at this particular time.

EMPLOYEE 1: If it's going to be me, I'll teach her all I know. I guess it's like you say—if she doesn't learn it, there will be somebody else to take her place.

SUPERVISOR:
(Reinforcement) Remember, the faster she learns it, the faster you get out of that job.

EMPLOYEE 1: I know that. I'll try my best to teach her.

SUPERVISOR:
(Reinforcement) I know you will, and I know she'll succeed because of the way you'll teach her.

(Action Step 5) I agree with you guys. This is going to be a big change, and it's going to take some getting used to. We are going to treat her like any other employee who comes to Ajax. And I know that it's going to take your full cooperation to make this change work and to keep the unit operating efficiently. Can I count on each of you?

WORK GROUP: Yes. OK. I'll try.

SUPERVISOR:
(Self-Esteem) Thanks, men. We've always been one of the best crews here, and I know we'll continue to be that.
(One week later.)

EMPLOYEE 1: Patsy, all you have to do to switch this instrument is just leave this knob here for a second and make sure it is going to hold. And don't try to switch it too fast.

EMPLOYEE 2: Another thing you have to do is keep a real close eye on it for any change.

PATSY: That makes sense. I understand.

SUPERVISOR:
(Action Step 6) What are you all doing here?

EMPLOYEE 1: Patsy just had a question about the instrument, and we're explaining it to her—we're showing her how we go from automatic to manual and vice versa. She's doing a real good job; everything's going along just fine.

SUPERVISOR:
(Reinforcement and Self-Esteem) Great! I'm glad everything is going along OK. Well, Patsy, you're in good hands. Just listen to what they have to say—I'm sure you'll do a fine job as an operator.

PATSY: I sure will.

SUMMARY

Change is among the most common management problems. Yet too often management is so concerned with the technical aspects of a change that it fails to consider the human relations problems which a change can generate. Most often employees resist change because it may hurt them economically, psychologically, or socially. Seemingly irrational attitudes and behaviors are symptoms of deeper problems, and these problems must be brought to the surface if they are not to undermine the change. Real problems must be brought out into the open, and management must level with employees. The objective is to provide employees with complete background information that leads to the change, share the details of the change, and establish two-way communication rather than attempt a one-way "sale" of the change.

It is advisable to elicit questions, concerns, objections, and suggestions for implementing the change. It is always advisable to be sensitive to the self-esteem issues that typically surround change.

14
CONCLUSION
A Case History and
Some Misconceptions

As has been previously pointed out, an increasing number of companies are teaching supervisory skills through the behavior modeling process. The six components of this design (cognitive presentation, behavior model, behavior rehearsal, feedback and reinforcement, transfer of training, and management reinforcement) can be used to develop a wide range of behavioral skills in the individual and then provide a mechanism for transferring those skills to the job. This change model can best be described in the context of a specific program implemented in a 700-employee manufacturing operation of a forest production company. The program was developed in response to a need for interpersonal problem-solving skills among first-level supervisors.*

In their research report *Improving Managerial Effectiveness through Behavioral Modeling*, Porras and Anderson point out that upper-level management in the operation had been involved in a series of diagnostic activities designed to determine the causes of decreased productivity in certain key departments. One of the most troubling areas of concern was the first-line supervisor–hourly employee interface.

---

*The program described here was developed by MOHR Development, Inc., Stamford, Connecticut, a private consulting company. The validation study cited was designed and implemented by Dr. Jerry I. Porras, associate professor of organizational behavior, Stanford University, Graduate School of Business, and Brad Anderson, organization development specialist, Champion International Corporation. The data were reported in an unpublished paper by Porras and Anderson, presented in April 1980 at the Graduate School of Business, Stanford University.

As supervisors faced substandard output in a particular area, they would typically handle the situation either by ignoring it or by confronting the employees with hostile and abusive language. Predictably, neither strategy led to improvement in employee performance. Plant management would then typically respond by attempting to persuade or pressure the first-level supervisors to deal with the interactions more effectively. However, the supervisors continued to ignore or exacerbate problems with hourly production workers because they lacked the behavioral skills required for these situations.

Another issue at the first-line supervisory level was of concern to production managers. For some time, supervisors had been complaining about feeling controlled and helpless in their jobs. To a large extent, these feelings were a result of what supervisors saw as the increasing power of the union. Supervisors who experienced these feelings usually found it much easier to ignore problems than to take the more punishing route of dealing with them and encountering grievances and hostile shop stewards as a consequence.

With this setting as a background, a behavior-modeling change design was selected. The objective was to impact supervisory behavior and organizational performance.

THE SKILL MODEL

The content of this program was designed around ten critical incident situations selected from a survey of all first-line supervisors in the company. The survey asked supervisors to identify the most difficult problems they faced in managing their subordinates. The results of the survey were fed back to plant managers, who then discussed the survey data and arrived at a final decision regarding the program's content. From this meeting, the ten most difficult and frequently encountered incidents were chosen. Each incident was dealt with in a module which consisted of the six phases of the modeling design.

Although each developmental module has a distinct focus, an underlying set of concepts was common across all modules. In essence, the primary goal was to help each participant learn a basic set of skills and an approach for using them that could be applied to solving a broad range of employee-related problems. Learning how to deal with the ten problems used as a focus for the overall program was a means for achieving the primary goal.

The general behavioral skills and problem-solving approach are based on a series of behavioral science principles drawn from social learning theory, communication theory, and participative management theory. The approach is shown in Exhibit 4.

THREE PHASES OF SUPERVISOR-EMPLOYEE INTERACTION

In a supervisor-employee interaction, the approach consists of three distinct phases. The first phase involves identifying the

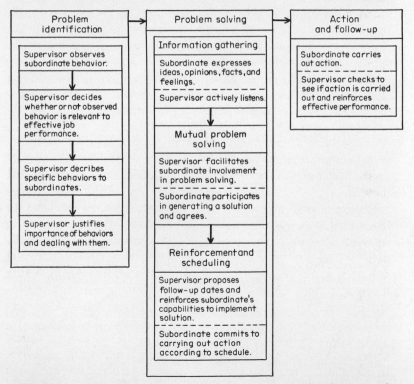

EXHIBIT 4 An approach to effective supervisor-subordinate problem-solving behavior.

problem to be solved; the second consists of a series of procedures for solving it; and the third involves implementing the desired solution. Each of these phases will be described in turn.

Problem Identification

This initial phase consists of four steps. In the first, the supervisor observes the specific behavior of the subordinate. In the second, the supervisor makes a judgment as to the relevance of the observed behavior to the employee's effectiveness. If the behavior is judged inappropriate, the supervisor takes the third step, which is to engage the subordinate in conversation and carefully describe the observed behavior. The supervisor, using the most important judgments made in the second step, attempts to be as precise in the description as possible. Next the supervisor explains why it is important to be discussing the behavior in the first place. In this fourth step the supervisor tries to increase the employee's awareness of the implications of his or her behavior and how the behavior fits into the wider work context. In so doing, the supervisor motivates the employee to become involved in the problem-solving process.

These early steps are designed to define the issue for the employee and to place it in its proper perspective. Their purpose is to facilitate the next phase, in which the employee presents his or her views. The supervisor and employee then begin to work out a collaborative solution to the problem situation.

Problem Solving

In this phase, the supervisor's first task is to generate information about the problem. Although the supervisor knows a good bit about the problem, there remains information which is known only by the subordinate. Therefore, the supervisor invites the subordinate to share his or her perspectives and responds by actively listening to *precipitate* a richer sharing of information by the employee. The supervisor tries to elicit not only the facts as seen by the employee but also the feelings the employee has about the problem situation. This occurs when the supervisor reflects back to the employee both the content of the message and the feelings behind it. This step, in conjunction with the previous phase, helps the supervisor obtain the data that is needed to effectively engage in mutual problem solving, the following step in this phase of the approach.

Next, the supervisor consciously tries to facilitate the involvement of the subordinate in problem solving. This is a key part of the procedure, for if it is done effectively, the subordinate will be most willing to implement the mutually agreed-upon solution.

Finally, the supervisor establishes a follow-up date for checking on the progress in implementing the desired solution. Further, the supervisor positively reinforces the employee by expressing confidence in the employee's ability to perform the action agreed on. In response, the employee makes a commitment to carrying out the agreed-upon action according to schedule.

Action and Follow-Up

In the last phase, the subordinate carries out the previously agreed-upon action and the supervisor monitors the progress. Effective performance is carefully reinforced by the supervisor so as to optimize the employee's willingness to repeat positive behaviors.

WORKSHOP CONTENT AND PROCEDURES

As a result of the survey of a company's supervisors, mentioned earlier, the following problem situations were chosen as topics for the various modules:

1. Motivating an employee who is having a performance problem

2. Handling employee complaints

3. Reducing resistance to change

4. Gaining the cooperation of another supervisor

5. Achieving a commitment to performance goals

6. Taking formal corrective action

7. Solving problems with your boss

8. Recognizing safe work practices

9. Improving performance through recognition

10. Improving attendance

Each participating group consisted of six to nine supervisors. The groups met once a week for approximately 6 hours and covered two skill modules per session. Since there was an introductory session to describe the basic skills used in the skill model plus a final wrap-up session, the program ran for a 7-week period.

The introductory session dealt with the purpose of the program, a brief overview of relevant theory, and skill practice exercises designed to help the participants develop the skills described in the change model. Following the introductory session, the change model was used as a basis for the ten skill modules.

Concept Generalization

In the final session—called "Model X"—the trainer asked all the participants to identify a new situation, one not covered in the ten modules, that was giving them difficulties on the job. The purpose of Model X was to help the participants generalize the basic approach learned during the course of the workshop. Some of the new situations identified by the supervisors were resolving conflict between employees, gaining the cooperation of the personnel department, and dealing with a suspected user of alcohol or drugs. The participants developed their own action steps for dealing with the particular situations they identified. The points were posted, participants engaged in behavior rehearsals, feedback was given, and contracts were made so that transfer occurred.

By developing their own action steps for dealing with a new situation, the participants proved to themselves that the approach acquired during the program could be applied to any problem involving an interpersonal encounter. In effect, Model

X demonstrated that what had been learned was not a cookbook approach but a general way of dealing with others—a process of engaging in a myriad of interactions.

Program Follow-Up

At the end of the program, the participants were asked to commit themselves to twenty new contracts and to document their experiences with these contracts during the next 2 months. The organization was concerned that if some form of follow-up wasn't implemented, a drop-off in the use of the skills might occur. Contract review sessions were to be held following the 2 months to (1) review the contracts that had been most successful and provide encouragement and reinforcement for the supervisors for using the skills, (2) review the contracts that had been less successful, and (3) discuss and decide upon other types of follow-up activities that would best ensure the continued use of the skills.

ORGANIZATIONAL SUPPORT

One added feature of this program should be discussed, as it relates to the issue of building organizational support for the new skills and behavior being developed by the supervisors. Workshop leaders were selected from line management positions, usually second- or third-level supervisors. An important reason for using production managers as leaders stemmed, in part, from the experience of the external consultants. These consultants had conducted programs themselves and then later heard that interest and enthusiasm had faded away soon after they had left.

Furthermore, by developing line managers as workshop leaders, the organization builds into its reward system a mechanism for communicating to its supervisors that the use of skills is desired and expected behavior. This was demonstrated in the opening session at the plant when a participant whose boss happened to be the session leader said, "I'm going to pay particular attention to what's going on." This type of response was rarely verbalized, but it serves to illustrate the high impact of this component of the design.

In addition to using line managers to conduct the program,

organizational support was developed by introducing the top management of the company to a shortened version. Top-level managers attended 1- to 2-day meetings to learn how they could reinforce others and encourage them to utilize the skills developed in the program. An important objective of these meetings was to gain the commitment of the top-level managers to the overall effort. The sessions were held for plant managers, general managers, and vice presidents in the manufacturing organization. Also included were all second-level supervisors not serving as workshop leaders. As a consequence, every manager in the organization associated with manufacturing was exposed to the content and process of the design. The value of these sessions was evidenced when second-level supervisors were observed asking their subordinate first-level supervisors to describe how they have been applying their skills on the job and then offering them encouragement and recognition for doing so.

PREDICTED OUTCOMES

It was expected that over a period of time the self-esteem of subordinates would increase as a result of the subordinates' being treated as important contributors to the effectiveness of the organization. And it was expected that the positive reinforcements used by supervisors to reward the productive behavior of subordinates would also serve to enhance the self-esteem of the individual employees.

In addition, it was expected that each supervisor's sense of efficacy would increase. As supervisors began to utilize their skills and find them to be effective, their feelings of mastery over the work environment would increase. As supervisors began to view themselves as more potent, their expectations about their ability to get the job done would be enhanced.

These changes in both supervisors and subordinates were then predicted to lead to improvements in individual and organizational efficiency and performance. Furthermore, solutions to subordinates' job-related problems such as absenteeism, turnover, tardiness, and grievance and accident rates were also expected.

EVALUATION OF THE PROGRAM

Plant performance data and labor relations data were collected along with perceptual data from plant personnel. A questionnaire based on the content and outcome models shown in Exhibit 4 was developed and administered to all supervisors participating in the program plus a stratified random sample of 30 percent of the employees reporting to each supervisor.

The supervisors were asked to provide information on their own attitudes, while hourly employees were asked to evaluate their supervisors' behavior. Questionnaires were administered 1 week before the program, 1 week after it ended, and 6 months later.

In essence, the research sought to determine whether supervisors changed their behavior in the following components of the model:

1. Behavior description to improve employee effectiveness

2. Justification of the need for action

3. Active listening

4. Participative problem solving that involves the employee

5. Positive reinforcement

Hourly employees responded to questions related to these and other key behaviors. Each question asked for the respondent's opinion of the extent to which the supervisor engaged in some specific behavior. Seven responses were possible, ranging from "Not at all" (1) to "To a very great degree" (7).

Behavior Change

The questionnaire results (Exhibit 5) show that at the most general level, supervisors significantly did change their behavior, as perceived by their subordinates.

A comparison of the measurements taken before and im-

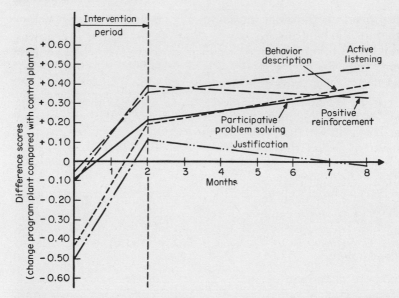

EXHIBIT 5 Supervisory behavior as perceived by subordinates: change program plant compared with control plant. (*Porras and Anderson, 1980.*)

mediately after the skill development sessions shows substantial changes in the five basic supervisory behaviors as perceived by the subordinates. Each of the reported changes is significant from a statistical point of view as well as from the perspective of absolute changes in the scaled responses.

When compared with the control plant, at the beginning of the research period, the change program supervisors, as a group, were less skilled in their use of the targeted behaviors. They began the program at levels which, in two cases, were substantially below those of the controls. Two months later, the change program supervisors were dramatically improved and were perceived to be using all the five skills at levels significantly above those of the controls. Their increased use of the skills was either maintained or further increased over the course of the succeeding 6 months. The only exception to this result was for justification; the final measurement was only slightly below that for the controls. However, even in this case, the drop was not down to preintervention levels, and, in fact, when considered in terms of overall change, justification behavior was the second best improved of the five basic skills.

The greatest overall change occurred in behavior description skills, which change program supervisors initially possessed at levels lower than those of the controls. By the end of the research period, these skills were among the highest for change plant supervisors. The least changed skill, but one which still improved significantly, was participative problem solving. Overall, it changed the least, yet it was one of three which showed an improvement between the postintervention and final measurements. The other two were behavior description and active listening.

At the last measurement, active listening was the skill used most by change program supervisors, while justification was least used. The remaining three were clustered together substantially above the controls at the final measurement. When considered from the point of view of change, all five skills were significantly improved.

The final measurements showed virtually no regression to preintervention levels. The changes reported immediately after the developmental workshops were essentially maintained. This is a particularly significant finding, since most change research tends to report an erosion of change if no concerted follow-on activities occur subsequent to the intensive phase of the intervention program. In the case reported here, two relatively short (2-hour) meetings were held with the supervisors. One occurred 2 months after the end of the workshops; the second, 4 months after. The purpose of these two sessions was to review progress and do additional rehearsal of needed skills.

In addition to the questionnaire data described above, other information on the impact of the program was secured through informal interviews with a cross section of the supervisors involved. One participant noted:

When I was made a supervisor, I had no idea how to approach

an employee whose performance was low. I really lacked confidence. This program has given me a way to structure my discussions, and I feel much more comfortable confronting an individual with a performance problem. The other day we had some safety equipment installed near one of the machines. Some of the employees weren't too happy with the change. Before the program, I would have said, "This is what the company wants whether you want it or not!" But instead I gave them the option of telling me how they felt about it. I was then able to explain the reasons for the change, and they seemed to be accepting it.

Another supervisor had an employee who had been absent 32 days in 3 months. All the absences were excused; the employee brought in statements from a doctor citing health reasons. Therefore, the supervisor felt that there was little that could be done. After going through the module on improving attendance, the supervisor decided to take action.

During our discussion I stuck to the learning points for improving attendance. I learned that this employee had been feeling a lot of stress because of the nature of his job. The reason he had missed so much was due to a bleeding ulcer. He hadn't talked about it before, and it was obvious that it was tearing him up to work on that job. We worked out a solution where I would put him on a less stressful job. He hasn't missed a day of work since then. I really think he appreciated being included in a discussion instead of being chewed out.

The general manager of this particular plant made the following observation regarding one of the supervisors: "Before the program, Jim was at a loss regarding how he should handle his people. This program has given him the opening line in his discussions and he is more effective and confident in his dealings with employees."

Another participant's reaction was: "It's helped me to keep my cool. I can recall several instances when I would have become angry and emotional without the training. Now I'm better able to stay calm and solve the problem."

A general observation from the supervisors who participated

in the program was that using the skills had dramatically opened up communication lines in terms of receiving suggestions from employees for improving productivity. One supervisor commented, "The employees feel like they have a voice. People are beginning to feel free to give you their ideas and we're following many of them." Another claimed, "The skills in this program have become a habit with me. Now that I've learned the basic skills involved, I make up my own guidelines according to the situation."

An unanticipated consequence of this program was described by one of the workshop leaders who noted that significant changes had occurred in the realm of supervisor-to-supervisor interaction. "The supervisors are cooperating with each other now. When supervisors have problems with one another, they don't hesitate to utilize their skills. It's made my job as their manager much easier."

Performance Change

All other things being equal, supervisory behavior, if changed in the direction of improved problem-solving skills, should lead to improved organizational performance. The impact of the change program on organizational productivity and efficiency was investigated by using three main indices of plant performance: (a) total monthly production per direct labor worker-hour, (b) average daily plant production, and (c) recovery rate (an index reflecting the degree to which a log is effectively converted into an end product).

Exhibit 6 shows the differences between change program plant and control plant performance indices for the research period. The performance indices shown are 6-month running averages. The actual figures have been disguised for proprietary reasons. However, the changes shown in the chart are proportionately accurate. Month 1 and 2 are the period during which the workshops were conducted.

Over the period of the research, the 6-month running average for total monthly production per direct labor worker-hour increased approximately 17 percent from the original level. The

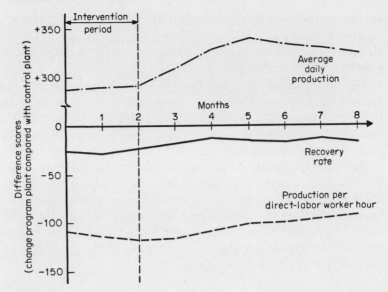

EXHIBIT 6 Organizational performance indices: change program plant compared with control plant. (*Porras and Anderson, 1980.*)

recovery rate relative to controls improved during the fourth month and through the seventh month at a rate equivalent to a decrease in costs of from $40,000 to $50,000 per month. Average daily production relative to controls increased approximately 25 percent in month 5 and then dropped off slightly, still remaining substantially above the rate prior to the beginning of the intervention.

All three indices of performance tend to indicate that changed supervisory behavior was leading to improvements in the performance of the organization. As supervisors became more effective in dealing with their subordinates, work productivity seemed to increase with corresponding increases in plant profitability.

Labor Relations Change

The changed supervisory behavior also appears to have had some effect on labor relations in the plant. (See Exhibit 7.) Three key measures were used to determine the impact in this area: (a) grievances rate, (b) absentee rate, and (c) turnover rate. For all three of these measures, the changes noted seemed to follow a general pattern of improvement.

The three graphs shown in Exhibit 7 are all 6-month running average differences between the change program plant and the control. Change plant turnover demonstrated the most substantial change, dipping to approximately four points below the control during the sixth month and then rising during the final 2 months. The absentee rate showed a steady decline, starting at two points above the control and then dropping until, during the seventh month, it fell below the control. The grievances rate was only slightly changed during the research period. Overall, the trends for both the turnover rate and the absentee rate were statistically significant, while grievances rate improvements were not. It appears that the improvements in supervisor be-

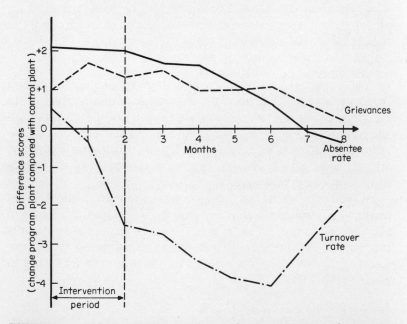

EXHIBIT 7 Labor relations indices: change program plant compared with control plant. (*Porras and Anderson, 1980.*)

havior reported earlier were associated with positive changes in two of the three key labor relations indices.

SUMMARY

Porras and Anderson conclude that the data very clearly indicate that the behavioral modeling–based intervention substantially affected the behavior of the first-line supervisors in the plant who participated in the experiment. Subsequent changes in plant performance and labor relations data indicate that the new problem-solving orientation of supervisors led to other, more profound improvements in plant efficiency and effectiveness. The researchers were left convinced that "behavior modeling is a powerful developmental technology and will find wide application to solving many of the human relations problems faced by managers."

While behavior modeling and supervisory skills training (SST) have achieved such concrete results as described in the above research, misconseptions about the process and the skills being taught have started to surface (Rosenbaum, 1979). Ten of these misconceptions and answers to them are listed in "Misconceptions about Behavior Modeling and SST."

Misconceptions are often a result of skepticism, and in the field of human resources development skepticism is understandable in view of its faddish history. However, the record so far suggests that we may have at last developed a meaningful learning model based on sound learning theory and research. In addition, we have recognized the value of converting theory and knowledge into skills and are now able to place the focus of training on the "bottom line," where it always belonged.

Misconceptions about Behavior Modeling and SST

Some of the misconceptions surrounding the application of the general principles and specific action steps as learned through the behavior modeling process are as follows.

1. It's soft management—a charm school—and that's not what our company needs.

   Answer: Quite the contrary. SST advocates that managers deal directly with employee problems as they arise. SST is as concerned with productivity as it is with any dimension of human relations. There is never a compromise on productivity for the sake of ensuring that people are happy. SST advocates focusing on behavior and dealing with specific performance problems. Consequently, it tends to be a tough approach, though it does teach managers to improve performance while maintaining the employees' self-esteem.

2. It's phony, and I don't feel sincere about using the principles of SST.

   Answer: At no time does the SST approach want managers to say things to an employee that they don't feel or believe. SST advocates being direct and specific. There is never anything that managers are asked to do that is insincere. However, SST teaches people new skills. Anytime people learn a new skill, it feels awkward. It is only with practice that the skill feels more natural. SST is designed to give managers that practice.

3. People are paid to do their jobs. Why baby them?

   Answer: A critical part of a supervisor's job is to create a climate that allows employees to do their best job. SST helps managers to more specifically define standards of performance and reinforce those employees who in fact are doing an excellent job. It also teaches supervisors to confront problems more directly.

4. What happens if there is no improvement? I guess then I can do it the old way.

   Answer: No. Managers can always use SST—right up to the time the employee is ushered out of the plant. SST is not just being nice to people. If necessary, managers can fire employees by using SST principles. Managers are direct and specific and do not compromise productivity. However, SST does not overcome selection problems. It relies on the premise that employees have the basic aptitudes to do their jobs. If they do not, it is an injustice to the employees as well as to the company to allow the situation to continue.

5. It's manipulative and sneaky.

Answer: If "manipulative" means that you're trying to modify, improve, and adjust behavior patterns, then yes—it is manipulative. But the word "manipulative" has a negative connotation: it implies deviousness and insincerity. SST advocates directness, not deviousness. It advocates letting people know where they stand. All SST principles and skills can be shared with employees. In fact, some companies are conducting formal SST orientations for employees.

6. It's trying to take away our personalities. Trying to make us all the same.

Answer: There are certain procedures we would like supervisors to gain some mastery of—just as they have acquired technical and administrative skills to do their job. Interpersonal skills help to maximize the productivity of people. However, each individual will use the skills in his or her own way. SST teaches skills; it does not change personalities.

7. SST assumes that all employees are alike.

Answer: It does make the assumption that all employees are alike in that it is based on the assumption that all normal, healthy employees have a need for self-esteem. Given this, SST places strong recognition on individual differences. In fact, a critical point that must be kept in mind is that one person's reward can often be another person's punishment. So a lot of attention must be paid to individual differences.

8. SST is OK, but we don't have time for it.

Answer: In a lot of situations it doesn't really take any longer. It reduces the variety of defensive behaviors that employees activate when they feel attacked and often saves time.

9. SST calls for clever, tricky, "psychological" ways of telling an employee about a problem.

Answer: In fact, most supervisors who have not been exposed to SST frequently go out of their way to find indirect methods of communicating problems to employees. For example, they make statements like "Don't you think there is a better way to do it?" Not only is this message indirect, it also tends to erode self-esteem. In SST the supervisor is asked to practice direct statements of problems rather than "beat around the bush."

10. Employees will know I'm using SST on them.

Answer: That's fine. There is nothing about SST that can't be shared with employees. In fact, it should be shared. Supervisors are encouraged to make statements like "I went to a training program. It covered a number of skills that I think can help us relate to each other. Let me tell you about some of the skills I've learned."

BIBLIOGRAPHY

Ardrey, R. *The Social Contract.* New York: Atheneum, 1970, p. 93.

Argyris, C. *Executive Leadership.* New York: Harper & Row, 1953, p. 13.

Berne, E. *Games People Play.* New York: Grove Press, 1964.

Blake, R. R., and Mouton, J. S. *The New Managerial Grid.* Houston: Gulf Publishing Company, 1978.

Coser, L. *The Function of Social Conflict.* Glencoe, Ill.: Free Press, 1954.

DeCharms, R. *Personal Causation: The Internal Affective Determinants of Behavior.* New York: Academic Press, 1968.

Festinger, L. A. *A Theory of Cognitive Dissonance.* Stanford, Calif.: Stanford University Press, 1957.

Goldstein, A. P., and Sorcher, M. *Changing Supervisor Behavior.* Elmsford, N.Y.: Pergamon Press, 1974.

Goldstein, I. L. Training in Work Organizations. *Annual Review of Psychology,* **31**:229–272 (1980).

Harris, T. *I'm OK—You're OK.* New York: Avon Books, 1973.

Herzberg, F. *Work and the Nature of Man.* Cleveland: World Publishing Company, 1966.

James, M., and Jongeward, D. *Born to Win.* Reading, Mass.: Addison-Wesley, 1971.

Korman, A. *Industrial and Organizational Psychology.* Englewood Cliffs, N.J.: Prentice-Hall, 1971, chap. 3, Motivational Factors in Work Performance.

Kuriloff, A. H. *Organizational Development for Survival.* New York: American Management Association, 1972.

Latham, G. P., and Locke, E. A. Goal Setting—A Motivational Technique That Works. *Organizational Dynamics,* autumn 1979, pp. 168–180.

Levinson, H. *Emotional Health in the World of Work.* New York: Harper & Row, 1964.

Livingston, J. S. Pygmalion in Management. *Harvard Business Review,* 1963.

Mager, R. F., and Pipe, P. *Analyzing Performance Problems.* Belmont, Calif.: Fearon Publishers, 1970.

Maslow, A. H. *Motivation and Personality.* New York: Harper & Row, 1954 (2d ed., 1970).

McGregor, D. *The Human Side of Enterprise.* New York: McGraw-Hill, 1960.

Porras, J. I., and Anderson, B. *Improving Managerial Effectiveness through Behavioral Modeling.* Unpublished Research Report, Stanford University, Graduate School of Business, 1980.

Rosenbaum, B. Common Misconceptions about Behavior Modeling and Supervisory Skills Training (SST). *Training and Development Journal,* August 1979.

Shaw, G. B. *Pygmalion* (edition bound with *My Fair Lady* by A. J. Lerner). New York: New American Library, 1975 (originally published 1912). Reprinted with permission of The Society of Authors on behalf of the Bernard Shaw Estate.

Sheppard, H. L., and Herrick, N. Q. *Where Have All the Robots Gone?* New York: Free Press, 1972.

Skinner, B. F. *About Behaviorism.* New York: Knopf, 1974.

Skinner, B. F. *The Behavior of Organisms.* New York: Appleton-Century-Crofts, 1938.

INDEX